Brian Friel was born in Omagh, Co. Tyrone, in 1929. His plays include *Philadelphia, Here I Come!*, *The Loves of Cass Maguire*, *Lovers*, *Freedom of the City*, *Volunteers*, *Living Quarters*, *Faith Healer*, *Translations* and *The Communication Cord*. In 1980 he founded the touring theatre company, Field Day, with Stephen Rea.

Michael Etherton, in *Contemporary Irish Dramatists* (Macmillan), writes:

Brian Friel is one of the most accomplished playwrights working in English today. His work is developed around a central poetic vision which has found, and enhanced, a language of theatre to communicate difficult ideas. This language of drama works through wider poetic sensibilities we actually share with the playwright but which we have lost sight of. Brian Friel sharpens our perceptions and makes us able to understand our human condition and the deepening ironies and contradictions of our age. This is his poetic vision.

DANCING
AT LUGHNASA

BRIAN FRIEL

faber and faber
LONDON · BOSTON

First published in 1990
by Faber and Faber Limited
3 Queen Square London WC1N 3AU

Photoset by Parker Typesetting Service Leicester
Printed in England by Clays Ltd, St Ives plc

A CIP record for this title is available from the British Library
ISBN 0–571–14479–9

6 8 10 9 7 5

In memory of those five brave Glenties women

CHARACTERS

MICHAEL, young man, narrator
KATE, forty, schoolteacher
MAGGIE, thirty-eight, housekeeper
AGNES, thirty-five, knitter
ROSE, thirty-two, knitter
CHRIS, twenty-six, Michael's mother
GERRY, thirty-three, Michael's father
JACK, fifty-three, missionary priest

MICHAEL, who narrates the story, also speaks the lines of the boy,
i.e. himself when he was seven.

ACT I
A warm day in early August 1936

ACT 2
Three weeks later

The home of the Mundy family, two miles outside the village of
Ballybeg, County Donegal, Ireland

SET

Slightly more than half the area of the stage is taken up by the
kitchen on the right. (Left and right from the point of view of the
audience.) The rest of the stage – i.e. the remaining area stage left
– is the garden adjoining the house. The garden is neat but not
cultivated.

Upstage centre is a garden seat.

The (unseen) boy has been making two kites in the garden and
pieces of wood, paper, cord, etc., are lying on the ground close to
the garden seat. One kite is almost complete.

There are two doors leading out of the kitchen. The front door
leads to the garden and the front of the house. The second in the

top right-hand corner leads to the bedrooms and to the area behind the house.

One kitchen window looks out front. A second window looks on to the garden.

There is a sycamore tree off right. One of its branches reaches over part of the house.

The room has the furnishings of the usual country kitchen of the thirties: a large iron range, large turf box beside it, table and chairs, dresser, oil lamp, buckets with water at the back door, etc., etc. But because this is the home of five women the austerity of the furnishings is relieved by some gracious touches – flowers, pretty curtains, an attractive dresser arrangement, etc.

Dress

Kate, the teacher, is the only wage-earner. Agnes and Rose make a little money knitting gloves at home. Chris and Maggie have no income. So the clothes of all the sisters reflect their lean circumstances. Rose wears wellingtons even though the day is warm. Maggie wears large boots with long, untied laces. Rose, Maggie and Agnes all wear the drab, wrap-around overalls/aprons of the time.

In the opening tableau Father Jack is wearing the uniform of a British army officer chaplain – a magnificent and immaculate uniform of dazzling white; gold epaulettes and gold buttons, tropical hat, clerical collar, military cane. He stands stiffly to attention. As the text says he is 'resplendent', 'magnificent'. So resplendent that he looks almost comic opera.

In this tableau, too, Gerry is wearing a spotless white tricorn hat with splendid white plumage. (Soiled and shabby versions of Jack's uniform and Gerry's ceremonial hat are worn at the end of the play, i.e. in the final tableau.)

Rose is 'simple'. All her sisters are kind to her and protective of her. But Agnes has taken on the role of special protector.

Dancing at Lughnasa was first performed at the Abbey Theatre, Dublin on 24 April 1990. The cast was as follows:

KATE	Frances Tomelty
MAGGIE	Anita Reeves
ROSE	Bríd Ní Neachtain
AGNES	Bríd Brennan
CHRIS	Catherine Byrne
MICHAEL	Gerard McSorley
GERRY	Paul Herzberg
JACK	Barry McGovern

Director	Patrick Mason
Designer	Joe Vanek
Lighting Designer	Trevor Dawson

This production transferred to the National Theatre in October 1990, with the following changes of cast:

KATE	Rosaleen Linehan
GERRY	Stephen Dillane
JACK	Alec McCowen

ACT 1

When the play opens MICHAEL *is standing downstage left in a pool of light. The rest of the stage is in darkness. Immediately* MICHAEL *begins speaking, slowly bring up the lights on the rest of the stage.*

Around the stage and at a distance from MICHAEL *the other characters stand motionless in formal tableau.* MAGGIE *is at the kitchen window (right).* CHRIS *is at the front door.* KATE *at extreme stage right.* ROSE *and* GERRY *sit on the garden seat.* JACK *stands beside* ROSE. AGNES *is upstage left. They hold these positions while* MICHAEL *talks to the audience.*

MICHAEL: When I cast my mind back to that summer of 1936 different kinds of memories offer themselves to me. We got our first wireless set that summer – well, a sort of a set; and it obsessed us. And because it arrived as August was about to begin, my Aunt Maggie – she was the joker of the family – she suggested we give it a name. She wanted to call it Lugh⋆ after the old Celtic God of the Harvest. Because in the old days August the First was *Lá Lughnasa*, the feast day of the pagan god, Lugh; and the days and weeks of harvesting that followed were called the Festival of Lughnasa. But Aunt Kate – she was a national schoolteacher and a very proper woman – she said it would be sinful to christen an inanimate object with any kind of name, not to talk of a pagan god. So we just called it Marconi because that was the name emblazoned on the set.

And about three weeks before we got that wireless, my mother's brother, my Uncle Jack, came home from Africa for the first time ever. For twenty-five years he had worked in a leper colony there, in a remote village called Ryanga in Uganda. The only time he ever left that village was for about six months during World War One when he was chaplain to the British army in East Africa. Then back to that grim

⋆*Lugh* – pronounced 'Loo'. *Lughnasa* – pronounced 'Loo-na-sa'.

I

hospice where he worked without a break for a further eighteen years. And now in his early fifties and in bad health he had come home to Ballybeg – as it turned out – to die.

And when I cast my mind back to that summer of 1936, these two memories – of our first wireless and of Father Jack's return – are always linked. So that when I recall my first shock at Jack's appearance, shrunken and jaundiced with malaria, at the same time I remember my first delight, indeed my awe, at the sheer magic of that radio. And when I remember the kitchen throbbing with the beat of Irish dance music beamed to us all the way from Dublin, and my mother and her sisters suddenly catching hands and dancing a spontaneous step-dance and laughing – screaming! – like excited schoolgirls, at the same time I see that forlorn figure of Father Jack shuffling from room to room as if he were searching for something but couldn't remember what. And even though I was only a child of seven at the time I know I had a sense of unease, some awareness of a widening breach between what seemed to be and what was, of things changing too quickly before my eyes, of becoming what they ought not to be. That may have been because Uncle Jack hadn't turned out at all like the resplendent figure in my head. Or maybe because I had witnessed Marconi's voodoo derange those kind, sensible women and transform them into shrieking strangers. Or maybe it was because during those Lughnasa weeks of 1936 we were visited on two occasions by my father, Gerry Evans, and for the first time in my life I had a chance to observe him.

The lighting changes. The kitchen and garden are now lit as for a warm summer afternoon.

MICHAEL, KATE, GERRY *and* FATHER JACK *go off. The others busy themselves with their tasks.* MAGGIE *makes a mash for hens.* AGNES *knits gloves.* ROSE *carries a basket of turf into the kitchen and empties it into the large box beside the range.* CHRIS *irons at the kitchen table. They all work in silence. Then* CHRIS *stops ironing, goes to the tiny mirror on the wall and scrutinizes her face.*

CHRIS: When are we going to get a decent mirror to see ourselves in?

MAGGIE: You can see enough to do you.

CHRIS: I'm going to throw this aul cracked thing out.

MAGGIE: Indeed you're not, Chrissie. I'm the one that broke it and the only way to avoid seven years bad luck is to keep on using it.

CHRIS: You can see nothing in it.

AGNES: Except more and more wrinkles.

CHRIS: D'you know what I think I might do? I think I just might start wearing lipstick.

AGNES: Do you hear this, Maggie?

MAGGIE: Steady on, girl. Today it's lipstick; tomorrow it's the gin bottle.

CHRIS: I think I just might.

AGNES: As long as Kate's not around. 'Do you want to make a pagan of yourself?'

(CHRIS *puts her face up close to the mirror and feels it*.)

CHRIS: Far too pale. And the aul mousey hair. Need a bit of colour.

AGNES: What for?

CHRIS: What indeed. (*She shrugs and goes back to her ironing. She holds up a surplice*.) Make a nice dress that, wouldn't it? . . . God forgive me . . .

(*Work continues. Nobody speaks. Then suddenly and unexpectedly* ROSE *bursts into raucous song*:)

ROSE: 'Will you come to Abyssinia, will you come?
    Bring your own cup and saucer and a bun . . .'

(*As she sings the next two lines she dances – a gauche, graceless shuffle that defies the rhythm of the song*.)

    'Mussolini will be there with his airplanes in the air,
    Will you come to Abyssinia, will you come?'

Not bad, Maggie – eh?

(MAGGIE *is trying to light a very short cigarette butt*.)

MAGGIE: You should be on the stage, Rose.

(ROSE *continues to shuffle and now holds up her apron skirt*.)

ROSE: And not a bad bit of leg, Maggie – eh?

MAGGIE: Rose Mundy! Where's your modesty!

(MAGGIE *now hitches her own skirt even higher than Rose's and does a similar shuffle*.)

Is that not more like it?

3

ROSE: Good, Maggie – good – good! Look, Agnes, look!

AGNES: A right pair of pagans, the two of you.

ROSE: Turn on Marconi, Chrissie.

CHRIS: I've told you a dozen times: the battery's dead.

ROSE: It is not. It went for me a while ago.

(*She goes to the set and switches it on. There is a sudden, loud three-second blast of 'The British Grenadiers'.*)

You see! Takes aul Rosie!

(*She is about to launch into a dance – and the music suddenly dies.*)

CHRIS: Told you.

ROSE: That aul set's useless.

AGNES: Kate'll have a new battery back with her.

CHRIS: If it's the battery that's wrong.

ROSE: Is Abyssinia in Africa, Aggie?

AGNES: Yes.

ROSE: Is there a war there?

AGNES: Yes. I've told you that.

ROSE: But that's not where Father Jack was, is it?

AGNES: (*Patiently*) Jack was in Uganda, Rosie. That's a different part of Africa. You know that.

ROSE: (*Unhappily*) Yes, I do . . . I do . . . I know that . . .

(MAGGIE *catches her hand and sings softly into her ear to the same melody as the 'Abyssinia' song:*)

MAGGIE: 'Will you vote for De Valera, will you vote?

   If you don't, we'll be like Gandhi with his goat.'

(ROSE *and* MAGGIE *now sing the next two lines together*:)

   'Uncle Bill from Baltinglass has a wireless up his —

(*They dance as they sing the final line of the song*:)

   Will you vote for De Valera, will you vote?'

MAGGIE: I'll tell you something, Rosie: the pair of us should be on the stage.

ROSE: The pair of us should be on the stage, Aggie!

(*They return to their tasks.* AGNES *goes to the cupboard for wool. On her way back to her seat she looks out the window that looks on to the garden.*)

AGNES: What's that son of yours at out there?

CHRIS: God knows. As long as he's quiet.

AGNES: He's making something. Looks like a kite.

4

(*She taps on the window, calls 'Michael!' and blows a kiss to the imaginary child.*)

Oh, that was the wrong thing to do! He's going to have your hair, Chris.

CHRIS: Mine's like a whin-bush. Will you wash it for me tonight, Maggie?

MAGGIE: Are we all for a big dance somewhere?

CHRIS: After I've put Michael to bed. What about then?

MAGGIE: I'm your man.

AGNES: (*At window*) Pity there aren't some boys about to play with.

MAGGIE: Now you're talking. Couldn't we all do with that?

AGNES: (*Leaving window*) Maggie!

MAGGIE: Wouldn't it be just great if we had a – (*Breaks off.*) Shhh.

CHRIS: What is it?

MAGGIE: Thought I heard Father Jack at the back door. I hope Kate remembers his quinine.

AGNES: She'll remember. Kate forgets nothing.

(*Pause.*)

ROSE: There's going to be pictures in the hall next Saturday, Aggie. I think maybe I'll go.

AGNES: (*Guarded*) Yes?

ROSE: I might be meeting somebody there.

AGNES: Who's that?

ROSE: I'm not saying.

CHRIS: Do we know him?

ROSE: I'm not saying.

AGNES: You'll enjoy that, Rosie. You loved the last picture we saw.

ROSE: And he wants to bring me up to the back hills next Sunday – up to Lough Anna. His father has a boat there. And I'm thinking maybe I'll bring a bottle of milk with me. And I've enough money saved to buy a packet of chocolate biscuits.

CHRIS: Danny Bradley is a scut, Rose.

ROSE: I never said it was Danny Bradley!

CHRIS: He's a married man with three young children.

ROSE: And that's just where you're wrong, missy – so there! (*To* AGNES) She left him six months ago, Aggie, and went to England.

5

MAGGIE: Rose, love, we just want –

ROSE: (*To* CHRIS) And who are you to talk, Christina Mundy! Don't you dare lecture me!

MAGGIE: Everybody in the town knows that Danny Bradley is –

ROSE: (*To* MAGGIE) And you're jealous, too! That's what's wrong with the whole of you – you're jealous of me! (*To* AGNES) He calls me his Rosebud. He waited for me outside the chapel gate last Christmas morning and he gave me this.

(*She opens the front of her apron. A charm and a medal are pinned to her jumper.*)

'That's for my Rosebud,' he said.

AGNES: Is it a fish, Rosie?

ROSE: Isn't it lovely? It's made of pure silver. And it brings you good luck.

AGNES: It is lovely.

ROSE: I wear it all the time – beside my miraculous medal. (*Pause.*) I love him, Aggie.

AGNES: I know.

CHRIS: (*Softly*) Bastard.

(ROSE *closes the front of her apron. She is on the point of tears. Silence. Now* MAGGIE *lifts her hen-bucket and using it as a dancing partner she does a very fast and very exaggerated tango across the kitchen floor as she sings in her parodic style the words from 'The Isle of Capri':*)

MAGGIE: 'Summer time was nearly over;
　　　Blue Italian skies above.
　　　I said, "Mister, I'm a rover.
　　　Can't you spare a sweet word of love?"'

(*And without pausing for breath she begins calling her hens as she exits by the back door:*)

Tchook-tchook-tchook-tchook-tchook-tchook-tchook-tchookeeeeeee . . .

(MICHAEL *enters and stands stage left.* ROSE *takes the lid off the range and throws turf into the fire.*)

CHRIS: For God's sake, I have an iron in there!

ROSE: How was I to know that?

CHRIS: Don't you see me ironing? (*Fishing with tongs.*) Now you've lost it. Get out of my road, will you!

AGNES: Rosie, love, would you give me a hand with this (*Of wool*). If we don't work a bit faster we'll never get two dozen pairs finished this week.

(*The convention must now be established that the* (*imaginary*) BOY MICHAEL *is working at the kite materials lying on the ground. No dialogue with the* BOY MICHAEL *must ever be addressed directly to adult* MICHAEL, *the narrator. Here, for example,* MAGGIE *has her back to the narrator.* MICHAEL *responds to* MAGGIE *in his ordinary narrator's voice.* MAGGIE *enters the garden from the back of the house.*)

MAGGIE: What are these supposed to be?

BOY: Kites.

MAGGIE: Kites! God help your wit!

BOY: Watch where you're walking, Aunt Maggie – you're standing on a tail.

MAGGIE: Did it squeal? – haaaa! I'll make a deal with you, cub: I'll give you a penny if those things ever leave the ground. Right?

BOY: You're on.

(*She now squats down beside him.*)

MAGGIE: I've new riddles for you.

BOY: Give up.

MAGGIE: What goes round the house and round the house and sits in the corner? (*Pause.*) A broom! Why is a river like a watch?

BOY: You're pathetic.

MAGGIE: Because it never goes far without winding! Hairy out and hairy in, lift your foot and stab it in – what is it? (*Pause.*)

BOY: Give up.

MAGGIE: Think!

BOY: Give up.

MAGGIE: Have you even one brain in your head?

BOY: Give up.

MAGGIE: A sock!

BOY: A what?

MAGGIE: A sock – a sock! You know – lift your foot and stab it – (*She demonstrates. No response.*)

D'you know what your trouble is, cub? You-are-buck-stupid!

BOY: Look out – there's a rat!

(*She screams and leaps to her feet in terror.*)

MAGGIE: Where? – where? – where? – Jesus, Mary and Joseph, where is it?

BOY: Caught you again, Aunt Maggie.

MAGGIE: You evil wee brat – God forgive you! I'll get you for that, Michael! Don't you worry – I won't forget that!

(*She picks up her bucket and moves off towards the back of the house. Stops.*)

And I had a barley sugar sweet for you.

BOY: Are there bits of cigarette tobacco stuck to it?

MAGGIE: Jesus Christ! Some day you're going to fill some woman's life full of happiness. (*Moving off*) Tchook-tchook-tchook-tchook . . .

(*Again she stops and throws him a sweet.*)

There. I hope it chokes you. (*Exits.*) Tchook-tchook-tchook-tchook-tchookeeeee . . .

MICHAEL: When I saw Uncle Jack for the first time the reason I was so shocked by his appearance was that I expected – well, I suppose, the hero from a schoolboy's book. Once I had seen a photograph of him radiant and splendid in his officer's uniform. It had fallen out of Aunt Kate's prayer book and she snatched it from me before I could study it in detail. It was a picture taken in 1917 when he was a chaplain to the British forces in East Africa and he looked – magnificent. But Aunt Kate had been involved locally in the War of Independence; so Father Jack's brief career in the British army was never referred to in that house. All the same the wonderful Father Jack of that photo was the image of him that lodged in my mind.

But if he was a hero to me, he was a hero and a saint to my mother and to my aunts. They pored over his occasional letters. They prayed every night for him and for his lepers and for the success of his mission. They scraped and saved for him – sixpence here, a shilling there – sacrifices they made willingly, joyously, so that they would have a little money to send to him at Christmas and for his birthday. And every so often when a story would appear in the *Donegal Enquirer* about 'our own leper priest', as they called him –

because Ballybeg was proud of him, the whole of Donegal was proud of him – it was only natural that our family would enjoy a small share of that fame – it gave us that little bit of status in the eyes of the parish. And it must have helped my aunts to bear the shame Mother brought on the household by having me – as it was called then – out of wedlock.

(KATE *enters left, laden with shopping bags. When she sees the* BOY *working at his kites her face lights up with pleasure. She watches him for a few seconds. Then she goes to him.*)

KATE: Well, that's what I call a busy man. Come here and give your Aunt Kate a big kiss.

(*She catches his head between her hands and kisses the crown of his head.*)

And what's all this? It's a kite, is it?

BOY: It's two kites.

KATE: (*Inspecting them*) It certainly is two kites. And they're the most wonderful kites I've ever seen. And what are these designs?

(*She studies the kite faces which the audience cannot see.*)

BOY: They're faces. I painted them.

KATE: (*Pretended horror*) Oh, good Lord, they put the heart across me! You did those? Oh, God bless us, those are scarifying! What are they? Devils? Ghosts? I wouldn't like to see those lads up in the sky looking down at me! Hold on now . . . (*She searches in her bags and produces a small, wooden spinning-top and whip.*) Do you know what this is? Of course you do – a spinning-top. Good boy. And this – this is the whip. You know how to use it? Indeed you do. What do you say?

BOY: Thanks.

KATE: Thank you, Aunt Kate. And do you know what I have in here? A new library book! With coloured pictures! We'll begin reading it at bedtime.

(*Again she kisses the top of his head. She gets to her feet.*)

Call me the moment you're ready to fly them. I wouldn't miss that for all the world.

(*She goes into the kitchen.*)

D'you know what he's at out there? Did you see, Christina? Making two kites!

CHRIS: Some kites he'll make.

9

KATE: All by himself. No help from anybody.

AGNES: You always said he was talented, Kate.

KATE: No question about that. And very mature for his years.

CHRIS: Very cheeky for his years.

ROSE: I think he's beautiful, Chris. I wish he was mine.

CHRIS: Is that a spinning-top he has?

KATE: It's nothing.

(MICHAEL *exits left.*)

CHRIS: Oh, Kate, you have him spoiled. Where did you get it?

KATE: Morgan's Arcade.

CHRIS: And I'm sure he didn't even thank you.

ROSE: I know why you went into Morgan's!

KATE: He did indeed. He's very mannerly.

ROSE: You wanted to see Austin Morgan!

KATE: Every field along the road – they're all out at the hay and the corn.

ROSE: Because you have a notion of that aul Austin Morgan!

KATE: Going to be a good harvest by the look of it.

ROSE: I know you have! She's blushing! Look! Isn't she blushing?

(CHRIS *holds up a skirt she is ironing.*)

CHRIS: You'd need to put a stitch in that hem, Rosie.

ROSE: (*To* KATE) But what you don't know is that he's going with a wee young thing from Carrickfad.

KATE: Rose, what Austin Morgan does or doesn't do with –

ROSE: Why are you blushing then? She's blushing, isn't she? Why-why-why, Kate?

KATE: (*Sudden anger*) For God's sake, Rose, shut up, would you!

ROSE: Anyhow we all know you always had a –

AGNES: Rosie, pass me those steel needles – would you, please? (*Pause.*)

CHRIS: (*To* KATE) Are you tired?

(KATE *flops into a seat.*)

KATE: That road from the town gets longer every day. You can laugh if you want but I *am* going to get that old bike fixed up and I *am* going to learn to ride this winter.

AGNES: Many about Ballybeg?

KATE: Ballybeg's off its head. I'm telling you. Everywhere you go – everyone you meet – it's the one topic: Are you going to the harvest dance? Who are you going with? What are you wearing? This year's going to be the biggest ever and the best ever.

AGNES: All the same I remember some great harvest dances.

CHRIS: Don't we all.

KATE: (*Unpacking*) Another of those riveting Annie M. P. Smithson novels for you, Agnes.

AGNES: Ah. Thanks.

KATE: *The Marriage of Nurse Harding* – oh, dear! For you, Christina. One teaspoonful every morning before breakfast.

CHRIS: What's this?

KATE: Cod-liver oil. You're far too pale.

CHRIS: Thank you, Kate.

KATE: Because you take no exercise. Anyhow I'm in the chemist's shop and this young girl – a wee slip of a thing, can't even remember her name – her mother's the knitting agent that buys your gloves, Agnes –

AGNES: Vera McLaughlin.

KATE: Her daughter whatever you call her.

ROSE: Sophia.

KATE: Miss Sophia, who must be all of fifteen; she comes up to me and she says, 'I hope you're not going to miss the harvest dance, Miss Mundy. It's going to be just *supreme* this year.' And honest to God, if you'd seen the delight in her eyes, you'd think it was heaven she was talking about. I'm telling you – off its head – like a fever in the place. That's the quinine. The doctor says it won't cure the malaria but it might help to contain it. Is he in his room?

CHRIS: He's wandering about out the back somewhere.

KATE: I told the doctor you thought him very quiet, Agnes.
(AGNES *had stopped knitting and is looking abstractedly into the middle distance.*)

AGNES: Yes?

KATE: Well, didn't you? And the doctor says we must remember how strange everything here must be to him after so long. And on top of that Swahili has been his language for twenty-five years; so that it's not that his mind is confused – it's just that he has difficulty finding the English words for what he wants to say.

CHRIS: No matter what the doctor says, Kate, his mind is a bit

confused. Sometimes he doesn't know the difference
between us. I've heard him calling you Rose and he keeps
calling me some strange name like –

KATE: Okawa.

CHRIS: That's it! Aggie, you've heard him, haven't you?

KATE: Okawa was his house boy. He was very attached to him.
(*Taking off her shoe*) I think I'm getting corns in this foot. I
hope to God I don't end up crippled like poor mother, may
she rest in peace.

AGNES: Wouldn't it be a good one if we all went?

CHRIS: Went where?

AGNES: To the harvest dance.

CHRIS: Aggie!

AGNES: Just like we used to. All dressed up. I think I'd go.

ROSE: I'd go, too, Aggie! I'd go with you!

KATE: For heaven's sake you're not serious, Agnes – are you?

AGNES: I think I am.

KATE: Hah! There's more than Ballybeg off its head.

AGNES: I think we should all go.

KATE: Have you any idea what it'll be like? – Crawling with
cheeky young brats that I taught years ago.

AGNES: I'm game.

CHRIS: We couldn't, Aggie – could we?

KATE: And all the riff-raff of the countryside.

AGNES: I'm game.

CHRIS: Oh God, you know how I loved dancing, Aggie.

AGNES: (*To* KATE) What do you say?

KATE: (*To* CHRIS) You have a seven-year-old child – have you
forgotten that?

AGNES: (*To* CHRIS) You could wear that blue dress of mine – you
have the figure for it and it brings out the colour of your eyes.

CHRIS: Can I have it? God, Aggie, I could dance non-stop all
night – all week – all month!

KATE: And who'd look after Father Jack?

AGNES: (*To* KATE) And you look great in that cotton dress you got
for confirmation last year. You're beautiful in it, Kate.

KATE: What sort of silly talk is –

AGNES: (*To* KATE) And you can wear my brown shoes with the
crossover straps.

KATE: This is silly talk. We can't, Agnes. How can we?

ROSE: Will Maggie go with us?

CHRIS: Will Maggie what! Try to stop her!

KATE: Oh God, Agnes, what do you think?

AGNES: We're going.

KATE: Are we?

ROSE: We're off! We're away!

KATE: Maybe we're mad – are we mad?

CHRIS: It costs four and six to get in.

AGNES: I've five pounds saved. I'll take you. I'll take us all.

KATE: Hold on now –

AGNES: How many years has it been since we were at the harvest dance? – at any dance? And I don't care how young they are, how drunk and dirty and sweaty they are. I want to dance, Kate. It's the Festival of Lughnasa. I'm only thirty-five. I want to dance.

KATE: (*Wretched*) I know, I know, Agnes, I know. All the same – oh my God – I don't know if it's –

AGNES: It's settled. We're going – the Mundy girls – all five of us together.

CHRIS: Like we used to.

AGNES: Like we used to.

ROSE: I love you, Aggie! I love you more than chocolate biscuits!
(ROSE *kisses* AGNES *impetuously, flings her arms above her head, begins singing 'Abyssinia' and does the first steps of a bizarre and abandoned dance. At this* KATE *panics.*)

KATE: No, no, no! We're going nowhere!

CHRIS: If we all want to go –

KATE: Look at yourselves, will you! Just look at yourselves! Dancing at our time of day? That's for young people with no duties and no responsibilities and nothing in their heads but pleasure.

AGNES: Kate, I think we –

KATE: Do you want the whole countryside to be laughing at us? – women of our years? – mature women, *dancing*? What's come over you all? And this is Father Jack's home – we must never forget that – ever. No, no, we're going to no harvest dance.

ROSE: But you just said –

KATE: And there'll be no more discussion about it. The matter's over. I don't want it mentioned again.

(*Silence.* MAGGIE *returns to the garden from the back of the house. She has the hen bucket on her arm and her hands are cupped as if she were holding something fragile between them. She goes to the kite materials.*)

MAGGIE: The fox is back.

BOY: Did you see him?

MAGGIE: He has a hole chewed in the henhouse door.

BOY: Did you get a look at him, Aunt Maggie?

MAGGIE: Wasn't I talking to him. He was asking for you.

BOY: Ha-ha. What's that you have in your hands?

MAGGIE: Something I found.

BOY: What?

MAGGIE: Sitting very still at the foot of the holly tree.

BOY: Show me.

MAGGIE: Say please three times.

BOY: Please-please-please.

MAGGIE: In Swahili.

BOY: Are you going to show it to me or are you not?

MAGGIE: (*Crouching down beside him*) Now, cub, put your ear over here. Listen. Shhh. D'you hear it?

BOY: I think so . . . yes.

MAGGIE: What do you hear?

BOY: Something.

MAGGIE: Are you sure?

BOY: Yes, I'm sure. Show me, Aunt Maggie.

MAGGIE: All right. Ready? Get back a bit. Bit further. Right?

BOY: Yes.

(*Suddenly she opens her hands and her eyes follow the rapid and imaginary flight of something up to the sky and out of sight. She continues staring after it. Pause.*)

What was it?

MAGGIE: Did you see it?

BOY: I think so . . . yes.

MAGGIE: Wasn't it wonderful?

BOY: Was it a bird?

MAGGIE: The colours are so beautiful. (*She gets to her feet.*) Trouble is – just one quick glimpse – that's all you ever get. And if you miss that . . .

(*She moves off towards the back door of the kitchen.*)

BOY: What was it, Aunt Maggie?

MAGGIE: Don't you know what it was? It was all in your mind. Now we're quits.

KATE: (*Unpacking*) Tea . . . soap . . . Indian meal . . . jelly . . .

MAGGIE: I'm sick of that white rooster of yours, Rosie. Some pet that. Look at the lump he took out of my arm.

ROSE: You don't speak to him right.

MAGGIE: I know the speaking he'll get from me – the weight of my boot. Would you put some turf on that fire, Chrissie; I'm going to make some soda bread.

(*Maggie washes her hands and begins baking.*)

ROSE: (*Privately*) Watch out. She's in one of her cranky moods.

KATE: Your ten Wild Woodbine, Maggie.

MAGGIE: Great. The tongue's out a mile.

ROSE: (*Privately*) You missed it all, Maggie.

MAGGIE: What did I miss this time?

ROSE: We were all going to go to the harvest dance – like the old days. And then Kate –

KATE: Your shoes, Rose. The shoemaker says, whatever kind of feet you have, only the insides of the soles wear down.

ROSE: Is that a bad thing?

KATE: That is neither a bad thing nor a good thing, Rose. It's just – distinctive, as might be expected.

(ROSE *grimaces behind* KATE'*s back.*)

Cornflour . . . salt . . . tapioca – it's gone up a penny for some reason . . . sugar for the bilberry jam – if we ever get the bilberries . . .

(AGNES *and* ROSE *exchange looks.*)

MAGGIE: (*Privately to* ROSE) Look at the packet of Wild Woodbine she got me.

ROSE: What's wrong with it?

MAGGIE: Only nine cigarettes in it. They're so wild one of them must have escaped on her.

(*They laugh secretly.*)

CHRIS: Doesn't Jack sometimes call you Okawa, too, Maggie?

MAGGIE: Yes. What does it mean?

CHRIS: Okawa was his house boy, Kate says.

MAGGIE: Dammit. I thought it was Swahili for gorgeous.

15

AGNES: Maggie!

MAGGIE: That's the very thing we could do with here – a house boy.

KATE: And the battery. The man in the shop says we go through these things quicker than anyone in Ballybeg.

CHRIS: Good for us.

(CHRIS *takes the battery and leaves it beside Marconi*.)

KATE: I met the parish priest. I don't know what has happened to that man. But ever since Father Jack came home he can hardly look me in the eye.

MAGGIE: That's because you keep winking at him, Kate.

CHRIS: He was always moody, that man.

KATE: Maybe that's it . . . The paper . . . candles . . . matches . . . The word's not good on that young Sweeney boy from the back hills. He was anointed last night.

MAGGIE: I didn't know he was dying?

KATE: Not an inch of his body that isn't burned.

AGNES: Does anybody know what happened?

KATE: Some silly prank up in the hills. He knows he's dying, the poor boy. Just lies there, moaning.

CHRIS: What sort of prank?

KATE: How would I know?

CHRIS: What are they saying in the town?

KATE: I know no more than I've told you, Christina.

(*Pause*.)

ROSE: (*Quietly, resolutely*) It was last Sunday week, the first night of the Festival of Lughnasa; and they were doing what they do every year up there in the back hills.

KATE: Festival of Lughnasa! What sort of –

ROSE: First they light a bonfire beside a spring well. Then they dance round it. Then they drive their cattle through the flames to banish the devil out of them.

KATE: Banish the – ! You don't know the first thing about what –

ROSE: And this year there was an extra big crowd of boys and girls. And they were off their heads with drink. And young Sweeney's trousers caught fire and he went up like a torch. That's what happened.

KATE: Who filled your head with that nonsense?

ROSE: They do it every Lughnasa. I'm telling you. That's what happened.

KATE: (*Very angry, almost shouting*) And they're savages! I know those people from the back hills! I've taught them! Savages – that's what they are! And what pagan practices they have are no concern of ours – none whatever! It's a sorry day to hear talk like that in a Christian home, a Catholic home! All I can say is that I'm shocked and disappointed to hear you repeating rubbish like that, Rose!

ROSE: (*Quietly, resolutely*) That's what happened. I'm telling you. (*Pause.*)

MAGGIE: All the same it would be very handy in the winter time to have a wee house boy to feed the hens: 'Tchook-tchook-tchook-tchook-tchook-tchook-tchook-tchookeeee . . . ' (FATHER JACK *enters by the back door. He looks frail and older than his fifty-three years. Broad-brimmed black hat. Heavy grey top coat. Woollen trousers that stop well short of his ankles. Heavy black boots. Thick woollen socks. No clerical collar. He walks – shuffles quickly – with his hands behind his back. He seems uneasy, confused. Scarcely any trace of an Irish accent.*)

JACK: I beg your pardon . . . the wrong apartment . . . forgive me . . .

KATE: Come in and join us, Jack.

JACK: May I?

MAGGIE: You're looking well, Jack.

JACK: Yes? I expected to enter my bedroom through that . . . what I am missing – what I require . . . I had a handkerchief in my pocket and I think perhaps I –

CHRIS: (*Taking one from the ironing pile*) Here's a handkerchief.

JACK: I thank you. I am grateful. It is so strange: I don't remember the – the architecture? – the planning? – what's the word? – the lay-out! – I don't recollect the lay-out of this home . . . scarcely. That is strange, isn't it? I thought the front door was there. (*To* KATE) You walked to the village to buy stores, Agnes?

KATE: It's Kate. And dozens of people were asking for you.

JACK: They remember me?

KATE: Of course they remember you! And when you're feeling stronger they're going to have a great public welcome for you – flags, bands, speeches, everything!

JACK: Why would they do this?

KATE: Because they're delighted you're back.

JACK: Yes?

KATE: Because they're delighted you're home.

JACK: I'm afraid I don't remember them. I couldn't name ten people in Ballybeg now.

CHRIS: It will all come back to you. Don't worry.

JACK: You think so?

AGNES: Yes, it will.

JACK: Perhaps . . . I feel the climate so cold . . . if you'll forgive me . . .

AGNES: Why don't you lie down for a while?

JACK: I may do that . . . thank you . . . you are most kind . . . (*He shuffles off. Pause. A sense of unease, almost embarrassment.*)

KATE: (*Briskly*) It will be a slow process but he'll be fine. Apples . . . butter . . . margarine . . . flour . . . And wait till you hear! Who did I meet in the post office! Maggie, are you listening to me?

MAGGIE: Yes?

KATE: You'll never believe it – your old pal, Bernie O'Donnell! Home from London! First time back in twenty years!

MAGGIE: Bernie . . .

KATE: Absolutely gorgeous. The figure of a girl of eighteen. Dressed to kill from head to foot. And the hair! – as black and as curly as the day she left. I can't tell you – a film star!

MAGGIE: Bernie O'Donnell . . .

KATE: And beside her two of the most beautiful children you ever laid eyes on. Twins. They'll be fourteen next month. And to see the three of them together – like sisters, I'm telling you.

MAGGIE: Twin girls.

KATE: Identical.

MAGGIE: Identical.

KATE: Nora and Nina.

ROSE: Mother used to say twins are a double blessing.

MAGGIE: Bernie O'Donnell . . . oh my goodness . . .

KATE: And wait till you hear – they are pure blond! 'Where in the name of God did the blond hair come from?' I asked her. 'The father. Eric,' she says. 'He's from Stockholm.'

18

AGNES: Stockholm!

ROSE: Where's Stockholm, Aggie?

KATE: So there you are. Bernie O'Donnell married to a Swede. I couldn't believe my eyes. But the same bubbly, laughing, happy Bernie. Asking about everybody by name.
(MAGGIE *goes to the window and looks out so that the others cannot see her face. She holds her hands, covered with flour, out from her body.*)

CHRIS: She remembered us all?

KATE: Knew all about Michael; had his age to the very month. Was Agnes still the quickest knitter in Ballybeg? Were none of us thinking of getting married? – and weren't we wise!

ROSE: Did she remember me?

KATE: 'Rose had the sweetest smile I ever saw.'

ROSE: There!

KATE: But asking specially for you, Maggie: how you were doing – what you were doing – how were you looking – were you as light-hearted as ever? Everytime she thinks of you, she says, she has the memory of the two of you hiding behind the turf stack, passing a cigarette between you and falling about laughing about some boy called – what was it? – Curley somebody?

MAGGIE: Curley McDaid. An eejit of a fella. Bald as an egg at seventeen. Bernie O'Donnell . . . oh my goodness . . .
(*Pause.*)

AGNES: Will she be around for a while?

KATE: Leaving tomorrow.

AGNES: We won't see her so. That's a pity.

CHRIS: Nice names, aren't they? – Nina and Nora.

KATE: I like Nora. Nice name. Strong name.

AGNES: Not so sure about Nina. (*To* CHRIS) Do you like Nina for a name?

CHRIS: Nina? No, not a lot.

KATE: Well, if there's a Saint Nina, I'm afraid she's not in my prayer book.

AGNES: Maybe she's a Swedish saint.

KATE: Saints in Sweden! What'll it be next!

ROSE: Mother used to say twins are a double blessing.

KATE: (*Sharply*) You've offered us that cheap wisdom already, Rose.

19

(Pause.)

CHRIS: You've got some flour on your nose, Maggie.

MAGGIE: When I was sixteen I remember slipping out one
Sunday night – it was this time of year, the beginning of
August – and Bernie and I met at the gate of the workhouse
and the pair of us off to a dance in Ardstraw. I was being
pestered by a fellow called Tim Carlin at the time but it was
really Brian McGuinness that I was – that I was keen on.
Remember Brian with the white hands and the longest
eyelashes you ever saw? But of course he was crazy about
Bernie. Anyhow the two boys took us on the bar of their
bikes and off the four of us headed to Ardstraw, fifteen miles
each way. If Daddy had known, may he rest in peace . . .

And at the end of the night there was a competition for the
Best Military Two-step. And it was down to three couples:
the local pair from Ardstraw; wee Timmy and myself – he
was up to there on me; and Brian and Bernie . . .

And they were just so beautiful together, so stylish; you
couldn't take your eyes off them. People just stopped
dancing and gazed at them . . .

And when the judges announced the winners – they were
probably blind drunk – naturally the local couple came first;
and Timmy and myself came second; and Brian and Bernie
came third.

Poor Bernie was stunned. She couldn't believe it. Couldn't
talk. Wouldn't speak to any of us for the rest of the night.
Wouldn't even cycle home with us. She was right, too: they
should have won; they were just so beautiful together . . .

And that's the last time I saw Brian McGuinness –
remember Brian with the . . . ? And the next thing I heard he
had left for Australia . . .

She was right to be angry, Bernie. I know it wasn't fair – it
wasn't fair at all. I mean they must have been blind drunk,
those judges, whoever they were . . .

*(MAGGIE stands motionless, staring out of the window, seeing
nothing. The others drift back to their tasks: ROSE and AGNES
knit; KATE puts the groceries away; CHRIS connects the battery.
Pause.)*

KATE: Is it working now, Christina?

20

CHRIS: What's that?

KATE: Marconi.

CHRIS: Marconi? Yes, yes . . . should be . . .

(*She switches the set on and returns to her ironing. The music, at first scarcely audible, is Irish dance music – 'The Mason's Apron', played by a ceili band. Very fast; very heavy beat; a raucous sound. At first we are aware of the beat only. Then, as the volume increases slowly, we hear the melody. For about ten seconds – until the sound has established itself – the women continue with their tasks. Then* MAGGIE *turns round. Her head is cocked to the beat, to the music. She is breathing deeply, rapidly. Now her features become animated by a look of defiance, of aggression; a crude mask of happiness. For a few seconds she stands still, listening, absorbing the rhythm, surveying her sisters with her defiant grimace. Now she spreads her fingers (which are covered with flour), pushes her hair back from her face, pulls her hands down her cheeks and patterns her face with an instant mask. At the same time she opens her mouth and emits a wild, raucous 'Yaaaah!' – and immediately begins to dance, arms, legs, hair, long bootlaces flying. And as she dances she lilts– sings–shouts and calls, 'Come on and join me! Come on! Come on!' For about ten seconds she dances alone – a white-faced, frantic dervish. Her sisters watch her.*

Then ROSE's *face lights up. Suddenly she flings away her knitting, leaps to her feet, shouts, grabs* MAGGIE's *hand. They dance and sing–shout together; Rose's wellingtons pounding out their own erratic rhythm. Now after another five seconds* AGNES *looks around, leaps up, joins* MAGGIE *and* ROSE. *Of all the sisters she moves most gracefully, most sensuously. Then after the same interval* CHRIS, *who has been folding Jack's surplice, tosses it quickly over her head and joins in the dance. The moment she tosses the vestment over her head* KATE *cries out in remonstration, 'Oh, Christina – !' But her protest is drowned.* AGNES *and* ROSE, CHRIS *and* MAGGIE, *are now all doing a dance that is almost recognizable. They meet – they retreat. They form a circle and wheel round and round. But the movements seem caricatured; and the sound is too loud; and the beat is too fast; and the almost recognizable dance is made grotesque because – for example – instead of holding hands, they have their arms tightly*) *around one another's neck, one another's waist. Finally* KATE, *who has been watching the scene with unease, with alarm, suddenly leaps to her feet, flings her head back, and emits a loud 'Yaaaah!'*

KATE *dances alone, totally concentrated, totally private; a movement that is simultaneously controlled and frantic; a weave of complex steps that takes her quickly round the kitchen, past her sisters, out to the garden, round the summer seat, back to the kitchen; a pattern of action that is out of character and at the same time ominous of some deep and true emotion. Throughout the dance* ROSE, AGNES, MAGGIE *and* CHRIS *shout – call – sing to each other.* KATE *makes no sound.*

With this too loud music, this pounding beat, this shouting – calling – singing, this parodic reel, there is a sense of order being consciously subverted, of the women consciously and crudely caricaturing themselves, indeed of near-hysteria being induced. The music stops abruptly in mid-phrase. But because of the noise they are making the sisters do not notice and continue dancing for a few seconds. Then KATE *notices – and stops. Then* AGNES. *Then* CHRIS *and* MAGGIE. *Now only* ROSE *is dancing her graceless dance by herself. Then finally she, too, notices and stops. Silence. For some time they stand where they have stopped. There is no sound but their gasping for breath and short bursts of static from the radio. They look at each other obliquely; avoid looking at each other; half smile in embarrassment; feel and look slightly ashamed and slightly defiant.* CHRIS *moves first. She goes to the radio.*)

CHRIS: It's away again, that aul thing. Sometimes you're good with it, Aggie.

AGNES: Feel the top. Is it warm?

CHRIS: Roasting.

AGNES: Turn it off till it cools down.

(CHRIS *turns it off – and slaps it.*)

CHRIS: Bloody useless set, that.

KATE: No need for corner-boy language, Christina.

AGNES: There must be some reason why it overheats.

CHRIS: Because it's a goddamn, bloody useless set – that's why.

ROSE: Goddamn bloody useless.

KATE: Are wellingtons absolutely necessary on a day like this, Rose?

ROSE: I've only my wellingtons and my Sunday shoes, Kate. And it's not Sunday, is it?

KATE: Oh, dear, we're suddenly very logical, aren't we?

MAGGIE: (*Lighting a cigarette*) I'll tell you something, girls: this Ginger Rogers has seen better days.

KATE: It's those cigarettes are killing you.

MAGGIE: (*Exhaling*) Wonderful Wild Woodbine. Next best thing to a wonderful, wild man. Want a drag, Kitty?

KATE: Go and wash your face, Maggie. And for goodness' sake tie those laces.

MAGGIE: Yes, miss. (*At window*) Where's Michael, Chrissie?

CHRIS: Working at those kites, isn't he?

MAGGIE: He's not there. He's gone.

CHRIS: He won't go far.

MAGGIE: He was there ten minutes ago.

CHRIS: He'll be all right.

MAGGIE: But if he goes down to the old well –

CHRIS: Just leave him alone for once, will you, please?

(MAGGIE *shrugs and goes out the back door. Pause.*)

KATE: Who's making the tea this evening?

AGNES: Who makes the tea every evening?

CHRIS: (*At radio*) The connections seem to be all right.

KATE: Please take that surplice off, Christina.

CHRIS: Maybe a valve has gone – if I knew what a valve looked like.

KATE: Have you no sense of propriety?

CHRIS: If you ask me we should throw it out.

AGNES: I'd be all for that. It's junk, that set.

ROSE: Goddamn and bloody useless.

KATE: (*To* AGNES) And you'll buy a new one, will you?

AGNES: It was never any good.

KATE: You'll buy it out of your glove money, will you? I thought what you and Rose earned knitting gloves was barely sufficient to clothe the pair of you.

AGNES: This isn't your classroom, Kate.

KATE: Because I certainly don't see any of it being offered for the upkeep of the house.

AGNES: Please, Kate –

KATE: But now it stretches to buying a new wireless. Wonderful!

AGNES: I make every meal you sit down to every day of the week –

KATE: Maybe I should start knitting gloves?

AGNES: I wash every stitch of clothes you wear. I polish your shoes. I make your bed. We both do – Rose and I. Paint the house. Sweep the chimney. Cut the grass. Save the turf. What you have here, Kate, are two unpaid servants.

ROSE: And d'you know what your nickname at school is? The Gander! Everybody calls you the Gander!

(MAGGIE *runs on and goes straight to the window.*)

MAGGIE: Come here till you see! Look who's coming up the lane!

AGNES: Who's coming?

MAGGIE: I only got a glimpse of him – but I'm almost certain it's –

AGNES: Who? Who is it?

MAGGIE: (*To* CHRIS) It's Gerry Evans, Chrissie.

CHRIS: Christ Almighty.

MAGGIE: He's at the bend in the lane.

CHRIS: Oh, Jesus Christ Almighty.

(*The news throws the sisters into chaos. Only* CHRIS *stands absolutely still, too shocked to move.* AGNES *picks up her knitting and works with excessive concentration.* ROSE *and* MAGGIE *change their footwear. Everybody dashes about in confusion – peering into the tiny mirror, bumping into one another, peeping out the window, combing hair. During all this hectic activity they talk over each other and weave around the immobile* CHRIS. *The lines overlap:*)

KATE: How dare Mr Evans show his face here.

MAGGIE: He wants to see his son, doesn't he?

KATE: There's no welcome for that creature here.

ROSE: Who hid my Sunday shoes?

MAGGIE: We'll have to give him his tea.

KATE: I don't see why we should.

MAGGIE: And there's nothing in the house.

KATE: No business at all coming here and upsetting everybody.

ROSE: You're right, Kate. I hate him!

MAGGIE: Has anybody got spare shoelaces?

KATE: Look at the state of that floor.

MAGGIE: Maybe he just wants to meet Father Jack.

KATE: Father Jack may have something to say to Mr Evans. (*Of the ironing*) Agnes, put those clothes away.

(AGNES *does not hear her, so apparently engrossed is she in her knitting.*)

MAGGIE: My Woodbine! Where's my Woodbine?

ROSE: He won't stay the night, Kate, will he?

KATE: He most certainly won't stay the night in this house!

MAGGIE: Have you a piece of cord, Aggie? Anybody got a bit of twine?

KATE: Behave quite normally. Be very calm and very dignified. Stop peeping out, Rose!

ROSE: (*At window*) There's nobody coming at all.
    (*Silence. Then* AGNES *puts down her knitting, rushes to the window, pushes* ROSE *aside and looks out.*)

AGNES: Let me see.

ROSE: You imagined it, Maggie.

CHRIS: Oh God.

ROSE: He's not there at all.

AGNES: (*Softly*) Yes, he is. Maggie's right. There he is.

ROSE: Show me.

KATE: Has he a walking stick?

ROSE: Yes.

KATE: And a straw hat?

ROSE: Yes.

KATE: It's Mr Evans all right.

AGNES: Yes. There he is.

CHRIS: Oh sweet God – look at the state of me – what'll I say to him? – how close is he?

ROSE: I couldn't look that man in the face. I just hate him – hate him!

KATE: That's a very unchristian thing to say, Rose. (*As* ROSE *rushes off*) There's no luck in talk like that!

CHRIS: Look at my hands, Kate – I'm shaking.
    (KATE *catches her shoulders.*)

KATE: You are not shaking. You are perfectly calm and you are looking beautiful and what you are going to do is this. You'll meet him outside. You'll tell him his son is healthy and happy. And then you'll send him packing – yourself and Michael are managing quite well without him – as you always have.
    (CHRIS *does not move. She is about to cry.* KATE *now takes her in her arms.*)
    Of course ask him in. And give the creature his tea. And stay

25

the night if he wants to. (*Firm again*) But in the outside loft.
And alone.
Now. I brought a newspaper home with me. Did anybody
see where I left it?
(CHRIS *now rushes to the mirror and adroitly adjusts her hair and
her clothes.*)

AGNES: Where is he, Maggie?

MAGGIE: In the garden.

KATE: Agnes, did you see where I left the paper?

MAGGIE: It's on the turf box, Kate.

(KATE *reads the paper – or pretends to.* AGNES *sits beside the
radio and knits with total concentration.* MAGGIE *stands at the
side of the garden window.* GERRY EVANS *enters left, his step
jaunty, swinging his cane, his straw hat well back on his head.
He knows he is being watched. Although he is very ill at ease the
smile never leaves his face.* CHRIS *goes out to the garden where
they meet.* GERRY *has an English accent.*)

GERRY: How are you, Chrissie? Great to see you.

CHRIS: Hello, Gerry.

GERRY: And how have you been for the past six months?

CHRIS: Thirteen months.

GERRY: Thirteen? Never!

CHRIS: July last year; July the seventh.

GERRY: Wow-wow-wow-wow. Where does the time go? Thirteen
months? Phew! A dozen times – two dozen times I planned a
visit and then something turned up and I couldn't get away.

CHRIS: Well, you're here now.

GERRY: Certainly am. And that was a bit of good fortune. Last
night in a bar in Sligo. Bump into this chappie with a brand
new Morris Cowley who lets slip that he's heading for
Ballybeg in the morning. Ballybeg? Something familiar
about that name! So. Here I am. In the flesh. As a matter of
interest. Bit of good luck that, wasn't it?

CHRIS: Yes.

GERRY: He just let it slip. And here I am. Oh, yes, wonderful
luck.

CHRIS: Yes.

   (*Pause.*)

MAGGIE: Looks terrified, the poor fella.

26

KATE: Terrified, my foot.

MAGGIE: Come here till you see him. Aggie.

AGNES: Not just now.

MAGGIE: I'm sure he could do with a good meal.

KATE: I'll give him three minutes. Then if she doesn't hunt him, I will.

GERRY: You're looking wonderful, Chrissie. Really great. Terrific.

CHRIS: My hair's like a whin-bush.

GERRY: Looks lovely to me.

CHRIS: Maggie's going to wash it tonight.

GERRY: And how's Maggie?

CHRIS: Fine.

GERRY: And Rose and Kate?

CHRIS: Grand.

GERRY: And Agnes?

CHRIS: Everybody's well, thanks.

GERRY: Tell her I was asking for her – Agnes.

CHRIS: I would ask you in but the place is –

GERRY: No, no, some other time; thanks all the same. The old schedule's a bit tight today. And the chappie who gave me the lift tells me Father Jack's home.

CHRIS: Just a few weeks ago.

GERRY: All the way from Africa.

CHRIS: Yes.

GERRY: Safe and sound.

CHRIS: Yes.

GERRY: Terrific.

CHRIS: Yes.

GERRY: Lucky man.

CHRIS: Yes.

(GERRY *uses the cane as a golf club and swings*.)

GERRY: Must take up some exercise. Putting on too much weight.

KATE: He's not still there, is he?

MAGGIE: Yes.

KATE: Doing what, in God's name?

MAGGIE: Talking.

KATE: Would someone please tell me what they have to say to each other?

MAGGIE: He's Michael's father, Kate.

KATE: That's a responsibility never burdened Mr Evans.

CHRIS: A commercial traveller called into Kate's school last Easter. He had met you somewhere in Dublin. He had some stupid story about you giving dancing lessons up there.

GERRY: He was right.

CHRIS: He was not, Gerry!

GERRY: Cross the old ticker.

CHRIS: Real lessons?

GERRY: All last winter.

CHRIS: What sort of dancing?

GERRY: Strictly ballroom. You're the one should have been giving them – you were always far better than me. Don't you remember? (*He does a quick step and a pirouette.*) Oh, that was fun while it lasted. I enjoyed that.

CHRIS: And people came to you to be taught?

GERRY: Don't look so surprised! Everybody wants to dance. I had thousands of pupils – millions!

CHRIS: Gerry –

GERRY: Fifty-three. I'm a liar. Fifty-one. And when the good weather came, they all drifted away. Shame, really. Yes, I enjoyed that. But I've just started a completely new career, as a matter of interest. Never been busier. Gramophone salesman. Agent for the whole country, if you don't mind. 'Minerva Gramophones – The Wise Buy'.

CHRIS: Sounds good, Gerry.

GERRY: Fabulous. All I have to do is get the orders and pass them on to Dublin. A big enterprise, Chrissie; oh, one very big enterprise.

CHRIS: And it's going all right for you?

GERRY: Unbelievable. The wholesaler can't keep up with me. Do you see this country? This country is gramophone crazy. Give you an example. Day before yesterday; just west of Oughterard; spots this small house up on the side of a hill. Something seemed just right about it – you know? Off the bike; up the lane; knocks. Out comes this enormous chappie with red hair – what are you laughing at?

CHRIS: Gerry –

GERRY: I promise you. I show him the brochures; we talk about

28

them for ten minutes; and just like that he takes four – one
for himself and three for the married daughters.

CHRIS: He took four gramophones?

GERRY: Four brochures!

(*They both laugh.*)

But he'll buy. I promise you he'll buy. Tell you this,
Chrissie: people thought gramophones would be a thing of
the past when radios came in. But they were wrong. In my
experience . . . Don't turn round; but he's watching us from
behind that bush.

CHRIS: Michael?

GERRY: Pretend you don't notice. Just carry on. This all his
stuff?

CHRIS: He's making kites if you don't mind.

GERRY: Unbelievable. Got a glimpse of him down at the foot of
the lane. He is just enormous.

CHRIS: He's at school, you know.

GERRY: Never! Wow-wow-wow-wow. Since when?

CHRIS: Since Christmas. Kate got him in early.

GERRY: Fabulous. And he likes it?

CHRIS: He doesn't say much.

GERRY: He loves it. He adores it. They all love school nowadays.
And he'll be brilliant at school. Actually I intended bringing
him something small –

CHRIS: No, no; his aunts have him –

GERRY: Just a token, really. As a matter of interest I was looking
at a bicycle in Kilkenny last Monday. But they only had it in
blue and I thought black might be more – you know – manly.
They took my name and all. Call next time I'm down there.
Are you busy yourself?

CHRIS: Oh, the usual – housework – looking after his lordship.

GERRY: Wonderful.

CHRIS: Give Agnes and Rose a hand at their knitting. The odd bit
of sewing. Pity you don't sell sewing-machines.

GERRY: That's an idea! Do the two jobs together! Make an
absolute fortune. You have the most unbelievable business
head, Chrissie. Never met anything like it.

(*She laughs.*)

What are you laughing at?

MAGGIE: You should see the way she's looking at him – you'd think he was the biggest toff in the world.

KATE: Tinker, more likely! Loafer! Wastrel!

MAGGIE: She knows all that, too.

KATE: Too? That's all there is.

MAGGIE: Come over till you see them, Agnes.

AGNES: Not just now.

GERRY: You'd never guess what I met on the road out from the town. Talk about good luck! A cow with a single horn coming straight out of the middle of its forehead.

CHRIS: You never did!

GERRY: As God is my judge. Walking along by itself. Nobody near it.

CHRIS: Gerry –

GERRY: And just as I was passing it, it stopped and looked me straight in the eye.

CHRIS: That was no cow you met – that was a unicorn.

GERRY: Go ahead and mock. A unicorn has the body of a horse. This was a cow – a perfectly ordinary brown cow except that it had a single horn just here. Would I tell you a lie?
(CHRIS *laughs*.)
Go ahead. Laugh. But that's what I saw. Wasn't that a spot of good luck?

CHRIS: Was it?

GERRY: A cow with a single horn? Oh, yes, that must be a good omen. How many cows like that have you ever met?

CHRIS: Thousands. Millions.

GERRY: Stop that! I'm sure it's the only one in Ireland; maybe the only one in the world. And I met it on the road to Ballybeg. And it winked at me.

CHRIS: You never mentioned that.

GERRY: What?

CHRIS: That it winked at you.

GERRY: Unbelievable. That's what made it all so mysterious. Oh, yes, that must be a fabulous omen. Maybe this week I'm going to sell a gramophone or two after all.

CHRIS: But I thought you – ?

GERRY: Look! A single magpie! That's definitely a bad omen – one for sorrow. (*His stick as a gun*) Bang! Missed. (*Mock*

serious) Where's my lucky cow? Come back, brown cow, come back!
(*They both laugh.*)

KATE: They're not *still* talking, are they?

MAGGIE: Laughing. She laughs all the time with him. D'you hear them, Aggie?

AGNES: Yes.

KATE: Laughing? Absolutely beyond my comprehension.

AGNES: Like so many things, Kate.

KATE: Two more minutes and Mr Evans is going to talk to me. Laughing? Hah!

GERRY: Thinking of going away for a while, Chrissie.

CHRIS: Where to?

GERRY: But I'll come back to say goodbye first.

CHRIS: Are you going home to Wales?

GERRY: Wales isn't my home any more. My home is here – well, Ireland. To Spain – as a matter of interest. Just for a short while.

CHRIS: To sell gramophones?

GERRY: Good God, no! (*Laughs.*) You'll never believe this – to do a spot of fighting. With the International Brigade. A company leaves in a few weeks. Bit ridiculous, isn't it? But you know old Gerry when the blood's up – bang-bang-bang! – missing everybody.

CHRIS: Are you serious?

GERRY: Bit surprised myself – as a matter of interest.

CHRIS: What do you know about Spain?

GERRY: Not a lot. A little. Enough, maybe. Yes, I know enough. And I thought I should try my hand at something worthy for a change. Give Evans a Big Cause and he won't let you down. It's only everyday stuff he's not so successful at. Anyhow I've still to enlist . . . He's still watching us. He thinks we don't see him. I wouldn't mind talking to him.

CHRIS: He's a bit shy.

GERRY: Naturally. And I'm a stranger to him practically . . . does he know my name?

CHRIS: Of course he knows your name.

GERRY: Good. Thanks. Well, maybe not so good. He's a very handsome child. With your eyes. Lucky boy.

31

(*'Dancing in the Dark' softly from the radio.*)

MAGGIE: Good for you, Aggie. What did you do to it?

AGNES: I didn't touch it.

KATE: Turn that thing off, Aggie, would you?

(AGNES *does not.*)

GERRY: You have a gramophone! I could have got it for you wholesale.

CHRIS: It's a wireless set.

GERRY: Oh, very posh.

CHRIS: It doesn't go half the time. Aggie says it's a heap of junk.

GERRY: I know nothing about radios but I'll take a look at it if you –

CHRIS: Some other time. When you come back.

(*Pause.*)

GERRY: And Agnes is well?

CHRIS: Fine – fine.

GERRY: Of all your sisters Agnes was the one that seemed to object least to me. Tell her I was asking for her.

CHRIS: I'll tell her.

(*They listen to the music.*)

GERRY: Good tune.

(*Suddenly he takes her in his arms and dances.*)

CHRIS: Gerry –

GERRY: Don't talk.

CHRIS: What are you at?

GERRY: Not a word.

CHRIS: Oh God, Gerry –

GERRY: Shhh.

CHRIS: They're watching us.

GERRY: Who is?

CHRIS: Maggie and Aggie. From the kitchen window.

GERRY: Hope so. And Kate.

CHRIS: And Father Jack.

GERRY: Better still! Terrific!

(*He suddenly swings her round and round and dances her lightly, elegantly across the garden. As he does he sings the song to her.*)

MAGGIE: (*Quietly*) They're dancing.

KATE: What!

MAGGIE: They're dancing together.

KATE: God forgive you!

MAGGIE: He has her in his arms.

KATE: He has not! The animal!

(She flings the paper aside and joins MAGGIE *at the window.)*

MAGGIE: They're dancing round the garden, Aggie.

KATE: Oh God, what sort of fool is she?

MAGGIE: He's a beautiful dancer, isn't he?

KATE: He's leading her astray again, Maggie.

MAGGIE: Look at her face – she's easy led. Come here till you see, Aggie.

AGNES: I'm busy! For God's sake can't you see I'm busy!

*(*MAGGIE *turns and looks at her in amazement.)*

KATE: That's the only thing that Evans creature could ever do well – was dance. *(Pause.)* And look at her, the fool. For God's sake, would you look at that fool of a woman? *(Pause.)* Her whole face alters when she's happy, doesn't it? *(Pause.)* They dance so well together. They're such a beautiful couple. *(Pause.)* She's as beautiful as Bernie O'Donnell any day, isn't she?

*(*MAGGIE *moves slowly away from the window and sits motionless.)*

GERRY: Do you know the words?

CHRIS: I never know any words.

GERRY: Neither do I. Doesn't matter. This is more important. *(Pause.)* Marry me, Chrissie. *(Pause.)* Are you listening to me?

CHRIS: I hear you.

GERRY: Will you marry me when I come back in two weeks?

CHRIS: I don't think so, Gerry.

GERRY: I'm mad about you. You know I am. I've always been mad about you.

CHRIS: When you're with me.

GERRY: Leave this house and come away with –

CHRIS: But you'd walk out on me again. You wouldn't intend to but that's what would happen because that's your nature and you can't help yourself.

GERRY: Not this time, Chrissie. This time it will be –

CHRIS: Don't talk any more; no more words. Just dance me down the lane and then you'll leave.

GERRY: Believe me, Chrissie; this time the omens are terrific! The omens are unbelievable this time!

(*They dance off. After they have exited the music continues for a few seconds and then stops suddenly in mid-phrase.* MAGGIE *goes to the set, slaps it, turns it off.* KATE *moves away from the window.*)

KATE: They're away. Dancing.

MAGGIE: Whatever's wrong with it, that's all it seems to last – a few minutes at a time. Something to do with the way it heats up.

KATE: We probably won't see Mr Evans for another year – until the humour suddenly takes him again.

AGNES: He has a Christian name.

KATE: And in the meantime it's Christina's heart that gets crushed again. That's what I mind. But what really infuriates me is that the creature has no sense of ordinary duty. Does he ever wonder how she clothes and feeds Michael? Does he ask her? Does he care?

(AGNES *rises and goes to the back door.*)

AGNES: Going out to get my head cleared. Bit of a headache all day.

KATE: Seems to me the beasts of the field have more concern for their young than that creature has.

AGNES: Do you ever listen to yourself, Kate? You are such a damned righteous bitch! And his name is Gerry! – Gerry! – Gerry!

(*Now on the point of tears, she runs off.*)

KATE: And what was that all about?

MAGGIE: Who's to say?

KATE: Don't I know his name is Gerry? What am I calling him? – St Patrick?

MAGGIE: She's worried about Chris, too.

KATE: You see, that's what a creature like Mr Evans does: appears out of nowhere and suddenly poisons the atmosphere in the whole house – God forgive him, the bastard! There! That's what I mean! God forgive me!

(MAGGIE *begins putting on her long-laced boots again. As she does she sings listlessly, almost inaudibly:*)

MAGGIE: ''Twas on the Isle of Capri that he found her

34

Beneath the shade of an old walnut tree.
        Oh, I can still see the flowers blooming round her,
        Where they met on the Isle of Capri.'
KATE: If you knew your prayers as well as you know the words of
        those aul pagan songs! . . . She's right: I am a righteous
        bitch, amn't I?
MAGGIE: 'She was as sweet as a rose at the dawning
        But somehow fate hadn't meant it to be,
        And though he sailed with the tide in the morning,
        Still his heart's in the Isle of Capri.'
        (MAGGIE *now stands up and looks at her feet.*)
        Now. Who's for a fox-trot?
KATE: You work hard at your job. You try to keep the home
        together. You perform your duties as best you can – because
        you believe in responsibilities and obligations and good
        order. And then suddenly, suddenly you realize that hair
        cracks are appearing everywhere; that control is slipping
        away; that the whole thing is so fragile it can't be held
        together much longer. It's all about to collapse, Maggie.
MAGGIE: (*Wearily*) Nothing's about to collapse, Kate.
KATE: That young Sweeney boy from the back hills – the boy who
        was anointed – his trousers didn't catch fire, as Rose said.
        They were doing some devilish thing with a goat – some sort
        of sacrifice for the Lughnasa Festival; and Sweeney was so
        drunk he toppled over into the middle of the bonfire. Don't
        know why that came into my head . . .
MAGGIE: Kate . . .
        (MAGGIE *goes to her and sits beside her.*)
KATE: And Mr Evans is off again for another twelve months and
        next week or the week after Christina'll collapse into one of
        her depressions. Remember last winter? – all that sobbing
        and lamenting in the middle of the night. I don't think I
        could go through that again. And the doctor says he doesn't
        think Father Jack's mind is confused but that his superiors
        probably had no choice but send him home. Whatever he
        means by that, Maggie. And the parish priest did talk to me
        today. He said the numbers in the school are falling and that
        there may not be a job for me after the summer. But the
        numbers aren't falling, Maggie. Why is he telling me lies?

Why does he want rid of me? And why has he never come out to visit Father Jack? (*She tries to laugh.*) If he gives me the push, all five of us will be at home together all day long – we can spend the day dancing to Marconi.

(*Now she cries.* MAGGIE *puts her arm around her.* MICHAEL *enters left.*)

But what worries me most of all is Rose. If I died – if I lost my job – if this house were broken up – what would become of our Rosie?

MAGGIE: Shhh.

KATE: I must put my trust in God, Maggie, mustn't I? He'll look after her, won't he? You believe that, Maggie, don't you?

MAGGIE: Kate . . . Kate . . . Kate, love . . .

KATE: I believe that, too . . . I believe that . . . I do believe that . . .

(MAGGIE *holds her and rocks her.*

CHRIS *enters quickly left, hugging herself. She sees the boy at his kites, goes to him and gets down beside him. She speaks eagerly, excitedly, confidentially.*)

CHRIS: Well. Now you've had a good look at him. What do you think of him? Do you remember him?

BOY: (*Bored*) I never saw him before.

CHRIS: Shhh. Yes, you did; five or six times. You've forgotten. And he saw you at the foot of the lane. He thinks you've got very big. And he thinks you're handsome!

BOY: Aunt Kate got me a spinning-top that won't spin.

CHRIS: He's handsome. Isn't he handsome?

BOY: Give up.

CHRIS: I'll tell you a secret. The others aren't to know. He has got a great new job! And he's wonderful at it!

BOY: What does he do?

CHRIS: Shhh. And he has bought a bicycle for you – a black bike – a man's bike and he's going to bring it with him the next time he comes.

(*She suddenly embraces him and hugs him.*)

BOY: Is he coming back soon?

CHRIS: (*Eyes closed*) Maybe – maybe. Yes! Yes, he is!

BOY: How soon?

CHRIS: Next week – the week after – soon – soon – soon! Oh, yes, you have a handsome father. You are a lucky boy and I am a very, very lucky woman.

(*She gets to her feet, then bends down again and kisses him lightly*.)
And another bit of good news for you, lucky boy: you have
your mother's eyes!

(*She laughs, pirouettes flirtatiously before him and dances into the
kitchen*.)
And what's the good news here?

MAGGIE: The good news here is . . . that's the most exciting turf
we've ever burned!

KATE: Gerry's not gone, is he?

CHRIS: Just this minute.

(AGNES *enters through the back door. She is carrying some roses*.)
He says to thank you very much for the offer of the bed.

KATE: Next time he's back.

CHRIS: That'll be in a week or two – depending on his
commitments.

KATE: Well, if the outside loft happens to be empty.

CHRIS: And he sends his love to you all. His special love to you,
Aggie; and a big kiss.

AGNES: For me?

CHRIS: Yes! For you!

MAGGIE: (*Quickly*) Those are beautiful, Aggie. Would Jack like
some in his room? Put them on his windowsill with a wee card
– 'ROSES' – so that the poor man's head won't be demented
looking for the word. And now, girls, the daily dilemma:
what's for the tea?

CHRIS: Let me make the tea, Maggie.

MAGGIE: We'll both make the tea. Perhaps something thrilling
with tomatoes? We've got two, I think. Or if you're prepared
to wait, I'll get that soda-bread made.

AGNES: I'm making the tea, Maggie.

CHRIS: Let me, please. Just today.

AGNES: (*Almost aggressively*) I make the tea every evening, don't I?
Why shouldn't I make it this evening as usual?

MAGGIE: No reason at all. Aggie's the chef. (*Sings raucously:*)
  'Everybody's doing it, doing it, doing it.
  Picking their noses and chewing it, chewing it, chewing
  it . . .'

KATE: Maggie, please!

MAGGIE: If she knew her prayers half as well as she knows the words of those aul pagan songs . . .
(*Now at the radio*) Marconi, my friend, you're not still asleep, are you?
(FATHER JACK *enters. He shuffles quickly across the kitchen floor, hands behind his back, eyes on the ground, as if he were intent on some engagement elsewhere. Now he becomes aware of the others.*)

JACK: If anybody is looking for me, I'll be down at the bank of the river for the rest of the . . .
(*He tails off and looks around. Now he knows where he is. He smiles.*)
I beg your pardon. My mind was . . . It's Kate.

KATE: It's Kate.

JACK: And Agnes. And Margaret.

MAGGIE: How are you, Jack?

JACK: And this is – ?

CHRIS: Chris – Christina.

JACK: Forgive me, Chris. You were only a baby when I went away. I remember Mother lifting you up as the train was pulling out of the station and catching your hand and waving it at me. You were so young you had scarcely any hair but she had managed to attach a tiny pink – a tiny pink – what's the word? – a bow! – a bow! – just about here; and as she waved your hand, the bow fell off. It's like a – a picture? – a camera-picture? – a photograph! – it's like a photograph in my mind.

CHRIS: The hair isn't much better even now, Jack.

JACK: And I remember you crying, Margaret.

MAGGIE: Was I?

JACK: Yes; your face was all blotchy with tears.

MAGGIE: You may be sure – beautiful as ever.

JACK: (*To* AGNES) And you and Kate were on Mother's right and Rose was between you; you each had a hand. And Mother's face, I remember, showed nothing. I often wondered about that afterwards.

CHRIS: She knew she would never see you again in her lifetime.

JACK: I know that. But in the other life. Do you think perhaps Mother didn't believe in the ancestral spirits?

38

KATE: Ancestral – ! What are you blathering about, Jack? Mother was a saintly woman who knew she was going straight to heaven. And don't you forget to take your medicine again this evening. You're supposed to take it three times a day.

JACK: One of our priests took so much quinine that he became an addict and almost died. A German priest; Father Sharpeggi. He was rushed to hospital in Kampala but they could do nothing for him. So Okawa and I brought him to our local medicine man and Karl Sharpeggi lived until he was eighty-eight! There was a strange white bird on my windowsill when I woke up this morning.

AGNES: That's Rosie's pet rooster. Keep away from that thing.

MAGGIE: Look what it did to my arm, Jack. One of these days I'm going to wring its neck.

JACK: That's what we do in Ryanga when we want to please the spirits – or to appease them: we kill a rooster or a young goat. It's a very exciting exhibition – that's not the word, is it? – demonstration? – no – show? No, no; what's the word I'm looking for? Spectacle? That's not it. The word to describe a sacred and mysterious . . . ? (*Slowly, deliberately*) You have a ritual killing. You offer up sacrifice. You have dancing and incantations. What is the name for that whole – for that – ? Gone. Lost it. My vocabulary has deserted me. Never mind. Doesn't matter . . . I think perhaps I should put on more clothes . . .

(*Pause.*)

MAGGIE: Did you speak Swahili all the time out there, Jack?

JACK: All the time. Yes. To the people. Swahili. When Europeans call, we speak English. Or if we have a – a visitor? – a visitation! – from the district commissioner. The present commissioner knows Swahili but he won't speak it. He's a stubborn man. He and I fight a lot but I like him. The Irish Outcast, he calls me. He is always inviting me to spend a weekend with him in Kampala – to keep me from 'going native', as he calls it. Perhaps when I go back. If you co-operate with the English they give you lots of money for churches and schools and hospitals. And he gets so angry with me because I won't take his money. Reported me to my superiors in Head House last year; and they were very cross –

oh, very cross. But I like him. When I was saying goodbye to him – he thought this was very funny! – he gave me a present of the last governor's ceremonial hat to take home with – Ceremony! That's the word! How could I have forgotten that? The offering, the ritual, the dancing – a ceremony! Such a simple word. What was I telling you?

AGNES: The district commissioner gave you this present.

JACK: Yes; a wonderful triangular hat with three enormous white ostrich plumes rising up out of the crown. I have it in one of my trunks. I'll show it to you later. Ceremony! I'm so glad I got that. Do you know what I found very strange? Coming back in the boat there were days when I couldn't remember even the simplest words. Not that anybody seemed to notice. And you can always point, Margaret, can't you?

MAGGIE: Or make signs.

JACK: Or make signs.

MAGGIE: Or dance.

KATE: What you must do is read a lot – books, papers, magazines, anything. I read every night with young Michael. It's great for his vocabulary.

JACK: I'm sure you're right, Kate. I'll do that. (*To* CHRIS) I haven't seen young Michael today, Agnes.

KATE: Christina, Jack.

JACK: Sorry, I –

CHRIS: He's around there somewhere. Making kites, if you don't mind.

JACK: And I have still to meet your husband.

CHRIS: I'm not married.

JACK: Ah.

KATE: Michael's father was here a while ago . . . Gerry Evans . . . Mr Evans is a Welshman . . . not that that's relevant to . . .

JACK: You were never married?

CHRIS: Never.

MAGGIE: We're all in the same boat, Jack. We're hoping that you'll hunt about and get men for all of us.

JACK: (*To* CHRIS) So Michael is a love-child?

CHRIS: I – yes – I suppose so . . .

JACK: He's a fine boy.

CHRIS: He's not a bad boy.

JACK: You're lucky to have him.

AGNES: We're all lucky to have him.

JACK: In Ryanga women are eager to have love-children. The more love-children you have, the more fortunate your household is thought to be. Have you other love-children?

KATE: She certainly has not, Jack; and strange as it may seem to you, neither has Agnes nor Rose nor Maggie nor myself. No harm to Ryanga but you're home in Donegal now and much as we cherish love-children here they are not exactly the norm. And the doctors says if you don't take exercise your legs will seize up on you; so I'm going to walk you down to the main road and up again three times and then you'll get your tea and then you'll read the paper from front to back and then you'll take your medicine and then you'll go to bed. And we'll do the same thing tomorrow and the day after and the day after that until we have you back to what you were. You start off and I'll be with you in a second. Where's my cardigan?

(JACK *goes out to the garden.* KATE *gets her cardigan.*)

MICHAEL: Some of Aunt Kate's forebodings weren't all that inaccurate. Indeed some of them were fulfilled before the Festival of Lughnasa was over.

She was right about Uncle Jack. He had been sent home by his superiors, not because his mind was confused, but for reasons that became clearer as the summer drew to a close.

And she was right about losing her job in the local school. The parish priest didn't take her back when the new term began; although that had more to do with Father Jack than with falling numbers.

And she had good reason for being uneasy about Rose – and, had she known, about Agnes, too. But what she couldn't have foreseen was that the home would break up quite so quickly and that when she would wake up one morning in early September both Rose and Agnes would have left for ever.

(*At this point in* MICHAEL'*s speech* JACK *picks up two pieces of wood, portions of the kites, and strikes them together. The sound they make pleases him. He does it again – and again – and again. Now he begins to beat out a structured beat whose rhythm gives him pleasure. And as* MICHAEL *continues his speech,* JACK *begins to shuffle–dance in time to his tattoo – his body slightly bent over, his eyes on the ground, his feet moving rhythmically. And as he dances–shuffles, he mutters – sings – makes occasional sounds that are incomprehensible and almost inaudible.* KATE *comes out to the garden and stands still, watching him.* ROSE *enters. Now* ROSE *and* MAGGIE *and* AGNES *are all watching him – some at the front door, some through the window. Only* CHRIS *has her eyes closed, her face raised, her mouth slightly open; remembering.* MICHAEL *continues without stopping:*)

But she was wrong about my father. I suppose their natures were so out of tune that she would always be wrong about my father. Because he did come back in a couple of weeks as he said he would. And although my mother and he didn't go through a conventional form of marriage, once more they danced together, witnessed by the unseen sisters. And this time it was a dance without music; just there, in ritual circles round and round that square and then down the lane and back up again; slowly, formally, with easy deliberation. My mother with her head thrown back, her eyes closed, her mouth slightly open. My father holding her just that little distance away from him so that he could regard her upturned face. No singing, no melody, no words. Only the swish and whisper of their feet across the grass.

   I watched the ceremony from behind that bush. But this time they were conscious only of themselves and of their dancing. And when he went off to fight with the International Brigade, my mother grieved as any bride would grieve. But this time there was no sobbing, no lamenting, no collapse into a depression.

(KATE *now goes to* JACK *and gently takes the sticks from him. She places them on the ground.*)

KATE: We'll leave these back where we found them, Jack. They aren't ours. They belong to the child.

(*She takes his arm and leads him off.*)

Now we'll go for our walk.

(*The others watch with expressionless faces.*)

ACT 2

Early September; three weeks later. Ink bottle and some paper on the kitchen table. Two finished kites – their artwork still unseen – lean against the garden seat.

    MICHAEL *stands downstage left, listening to* MAGGIE *as she approaches, singing. Now she enters left carrying two zinc buckets of water. She is dressed as she was in Act 1. She sings in her usual parodic style:*

MAGGIE: 'Oh play to me, Gypsy;
      The moon's high above.
      Oh, play me your seranade,
      The song I love . . .'
    (*She goes into the kitchen and from her zinc buckets she fills the kettle and the saucepan on the range. She looks over at the writing materials.*)
    Are you getting your books ready for school again?
BOY: School doesn't start for another ten days.
MAGGIE: God, I always hated school.
    (*She hums the next line of the song. Then she remembers:*)
    You and I have a little financial matter to discuss. (*Pause.*)
    D'you hear me, cub?
BOY: I'm not listening.
MAGGIE: You owe me money.
BOY: I do not.
MAGGIE: Oh, yes, you do. Three weeks ago I bet you a penny
    those aul kites would never get off the ground. And they
    never did.
BOY: Because there was never enough wind; that's why.
MAGGIE: Enough wind! Would you listen to him. A hurricane
    wouldn't shift those things. Anyhow a debt is a debt. One
    penny please at your convenience. Or the equivalent in kind:
    one Wild Woodbine.
    (*Sings:*) 'Beside your caravan
      The campfire's bright . . .'
    (*She dances her exaggerated dance across to the table and tousles*

the BOY's *hair*.)

BOY: Leave me alone, Aunt Maggie.

MAGGIE: 'I'll be your vagabond
      Just for tonight . . .'

BOY: Now look at what you made me do! The page is all blotted!

MAGGIE: Your frank opinion, cub: am I vagabond material?

BOY: Get out of my road, will you? I'm trying to write a letter.

MAGGIE: Who to? That's for me to know and you to find out.
      Whoever it is, he'd need to be smart to read that scrawl.
      (*She returns to her buckets*.)

BOY: It's to Santa Claus.

MAGGIE: In September? Nothing like getting in before the rush.
      What are you asking for?

BOY: A bell.

MAGGIE: A bell.

BOY: For my bicycle.

MAGGIE: For your bicycle.

BOY: The bike my daddy has bought me – stupid!

MAGGIE: Your daddy has bought you a bicycle?

BOY: He told me today. He bought it in Kilkenny. So there!
      (*Her manner changes. She returns to the table*.)

MAGGIE: (*Softly*) Your daddy told you that?

BOY: Ask him yourself. It's coming next week. It's a black bike –
      a man's bike.

MAGGIE: Aren't you the lucky boy?

BOY: It's going to be delivered here to the house. He promised
      me.

MAGGIE: Well, if he promised you . . . (*Very brisk*) Now! Who can
      we get to teach you to ride?

BOY: I know how to ride!

MAGGIE: You don't.

BOY: I learned at school last Easter. So there! But you can't ride.

MAGGIE: I can so.

BOY: I know you can't.

MAGGIE: Maybe not by myself. But put me on the bar, cub –
      magnificent!

BOY: You never sat on the bar of a bike in your life, Aunt Maggie!

MAGGIE: Oh yes, I did, Michael. Oh yes, indeed I did. (*She
      gathers up the papers*.) Now away and write to Santa some

44

other time. On a day like this you should be out running about the fields like a young calf. Hold on – a new riddle for you.

BOY: Give up.

MAGGIE: A man goes to an apple tree with two apples on it. He doesn't take apples off it. He doesn't leave apples on it. How does he do that?

BOY: Give up.

MAGGIE: Think, will you!

BOY: Give up.

MAGGIE: Well, since you don't know, I will tell you. He takes *one* apple off! Get it? He doesn't take *apples* off!
He doesn't leave *apples* on!

BOY: God!

MAGGIE: You might as well be talking to a turf stack.
(JACK *enters. He looks much stronger and is very sprightly and alert. He is not wearing the top coat or the hat but instead a garish-coloured – probably a sister's – sweater. His dress looks now even more bizarre.*)

JACK: Did I hear the church bell ringing?

MAGGIE: A big posh wedding today.

JACK: Not one of my sisters?

MAGGIE: No such luck. A man called Austin Morgan and a girl from Carrickfad.

JACK: Austin Morgan – should I know that name?

MAGGIE: I don't think so. They own the Arcade in the town. And how are you today?

JACK: Cold as usual, Maggie. And complaining about it as usual.
(MICHAEL *exits.*)

MAGGIE: Complain away – why wouldn't you? And it is getting colder. But you're looking stronger every day, Jack.

JACK: I feel stronger, too. Now! Off for my last walk of the day.

MAGGIE: Number three?

JACK: Number four! Down past the clothes line; across the stream; round the old well; and up through the meadow. And when that's done Kate won't have to nag at me – nag? – nag? – sounds funny – something wrong with that – nag? – that's not a word, is it?

MAGGIE: Nag – yes; to keep on at somebody.

45

JACK: Yes? Nag. Good. So my English vocabulary is coming back, too. Great. Nag. Still sounds a bit strange.

(KATE *enters with an armful of clothes from the clothes line*.)

KATE: Time for another walk, Jack.

JACK: Just about to set out on number four, Kate. And thank you for keeping at me.

KATE: No sign of Rose and Agnes yet?

MAGGIE: They said they'd be back for tea. (*To* JACK) They're away picking bilberries.

KATE: (*To* JACK) You used to pick bilberries. Do you remember?

JACK: Down beside the old quarry?

MAGGIE: The very place.

JACK: Mother and myself; every Lughnasa; the annual ritual. Of course I remember. And then she'd make the most wonderful jam. And that's what you took to school with you every day all through the winter: a piece of soda bread and bilberry jam.

MAGGIE: But no butter.

JACK: Except on special occasions when you got scones and for some reason they were always buttered. I must walk down to that old quarry one of these days.

'O ruddier than the cherry,
O sweeter than the berry,
O nymph more bright,
Than moonshine night,
Like kidlings blithe and merry.'

(*Laughs*.) Where on earth did that come from? You see, Kate, it's all coming back to me.

KATE: So you'll soon begin saying Mass again?

JACK: Yes, indeed.

MAGGIE: Here in the house?

JACK: Why not? Perhaps I'll start next Monday. The neighbours would join us, wouldn't they?

KATE: They surely would. A lot of them have been asking me already.

JACK: How will we let them know?

MAGGIE: I wouldn't worry about that. Word gets about very quickly.

JACK: What Okawa does – you know Okawa, don't you?

MAGGIE: Your house boy?

JACK: My friend – my mentor – my counsellor – and yes, my house boy as well; anyhow Okawa summons our people by striking a huge iron gong. Did you hear that wedding bell this morning, Kate?

KATE: Yes.

JACK: Well, Okawa's gong would carry four times as far as that. But if it's one of the bigger ceremonies, he'll spend a whole day going round all the neighbouring villages, blowing on this enormous flute he made himself.

MAGGIE: And they all meet in your church?

JACK: When I had a church. Now we gather in the common in the middle of the village. If it's an important ceremony, you would have up to three or four hundred people.

KATE: All gathered together for Mass?

JACK: Maybe. Or maybe to offer sacrifice to Obi, our Great Goddess of the Earth, so that the crops will flourish. Or maybe to get in touch with our departed fathers for their advice and wisdom. Or maybe to thank the spirits of our tribe if they have been good to us; or to appease them if they're angry. I complain to Okawa that our calendar of ceremonies gets fuller every year. Now at this time of year over there – at the Ugandan harvest time – we have two very wonderful ceremonies: the Festival of the New Yam and the Festival of the Sweet Casava; and they're both dedicated to our Great Goddess, Obi –

KATE: But these aren't Christian ceremonies, Jack, are they?

JACK: Oh, no. The Ryangans have always been faithful to their own beliefs – like these two Festivals I'm telling you about; and they are very special, really magnificent ceremonies. I haven't described those two Festivals to you before, have I?

KATE: Not to me.

JACK: Well, they begin very formally, very solemnly with the ritual sacrifice of a fowl or a goat or a calf down at the bank of the river. Then the ceremonial cutting and anointing of the first yams and the first casava; and we pass these round in huge wooden bowls. Then the incantation – a chant, really – that expresses our gratitude and that also acts as a rhythm or

47

percussion for the ritual dance. And then, when the thanksgiving is over, the dance continues. And the interesting thing is that it grows naturally into a secular celebration; so that almost imperceptibly the religious ceremony ends and the community celebration takes over. And that part of the ceremony is a real spectacle. We light fires round the periphery of the circle; and we paint our faces with coloured powders; and we sing local songs; and we drink palm wine. And then we dance – and dance – and dance – children, men, women, most of them lepers, many of them with misshapen limbs, with missing limbs – dancing, believe it or not, for days on end! It is the most wonderful sight you have ever seen! (*Laughs.*) That palm wine! They dole it out in horns! You lose all sense of time . . . !

Oh, yes, the Ryangans are a remarkable people: there is no distinction between the religious and the secular in their culture. And of course their capacity for fun, for laughing, for practical jokes – they've such open hearts! In some respects they're not unlike us. You'd love them, Maggie. You should come back with me!

How did I get into all that? You must stop me telling these long stories. Exercise time! I'll be back in ten minutes; and only last week it took me half an hour to do number four. You've done a great job with me, Kate. So please do keep nagging at me.

(*He moves off – then stops.*)

It's not Gilbert and Sullivan, is it?

KATE: Sorry?

JACK: That quotation.

KATE: What's that, Jack?

JACK: 'O ruddier than the cherry / O sweeter than the berry' – no, it's not Gilbert and Sullivan. But it'll come back to me, I promise you. It's all coming back.

(*Again he moves off.*)

KATE: Jack.

JACK: Yes?

KATE: You are going to start saying Mass again?

JACK: We've agreed on next Monday, haven't we? Haven't we, Maggie?

48

MAGGIE: Yes.

JACK: At first light. The moment Rose's white cock crows. A harvest ceremony. You'll have to find a big gong somewhere, Kate.

(*He leaves. Pause.* KATE *and* MAGGIE *stare at each other in concern, in alarm. They speak in hushed voices.*)

KATE: I told you – you wouldn't believe me – I told you.

MAGGIE: Shhh.

KATE: What do you think?

MAGGIE: He's not back a month yet.

KATE: Yesterday I heard about their medicine man who brought a woman back from death –

MAGGIE: He needs more time.

KATE: And this morning it was 'the spirits of the tribe'! And when I mentioned Mass to him you saw how he dodged about.

MAGGIE: He said he'd say Mass next Monday, Kate.

KATE: No, he won't. You know he won't. He's changed, Maggie.

MAGGIE: In another month, he'll be –

KATE: Completely changed. He's not our Jack at all. And it's what he's changed into that frightens me.

MAGGIE: Doesn't frighten me.

KATE: If you saw your face . . . of course it does . . . Oh, dear God –

(MAGGIE *now drifts back to the range.* KATE *goes to the table and with excessive vigour wipes it with a damp cloth. Then she stops suddenly, slumps into a seat and covers her face with her hands.* MAGGIE *watches her, then goes to her. She stands behind her and holds her shoulders with her hands.* KATE *grasps* MAGGIE's *hands in hers.*)

MAGGIE: All the same, Kitty, I don't think it's a sight I'd like to see.

KATE: What sight?

MAGGIE: A clatter of lepers trying to do the Military Two-step.

KATE: God forgive you, Maggie Mundy! The poor creatures are as entitled to –

(*She breaks off because* CHRIS's *laughter is heard off.* KATE *jumps to her feet.*)

This must be kept in the family, Maggie! Not a word of this must go outside these walls – d'you hear? – not a syllable!

49

(CHRIS *and* GERRY *enter left. He enters backways, pulling* CHRIS *who holds the end of his walking stick. Throughout the scene he keeps trying to embrace her. She keeps avoiding him.*)

GERRY: No false modesty. You know you're a great dancer, Chrissie.

CHRIS: No, I'm not.

GERRY: You should be a professional dancer.

CHRIS: You're talking rubbish.

GERRY: Let's dance round the garden again.

CHRIS: We've done that; and down the lane and up again – without music. And that's enough for one day. Tell me about signing up. Was it really in a church?

GERRY: I'm telling you – it was unbelievable.

CHRIS: It was a real church?

GERRY: A Catholic church as a matter of interest.

CHRIS: I don't believe a word of it.

GERRY: Would I tell you a lie? And up at the end – in the sanctuary? – there were three men, two of them with trench-coats; and between them, behind this lectern and wearing a sort of military cap, this little chappie who spoke in an accent I could hardly understand. Naturally I thought he was Spanish. From Armagh, as it turned out.

CHRIS: I'm sure he couldn't understand you either.

GERRY: He described himself as the recruiting officer. 'Take it from me, comrade, nobody joins the Brigade without my unanimity.'

(*She laughs – and avoids his embrace.*)

CHRIS: It's a wonder he accepted you.

GERRY: 'Do you offer your allegiance and your loyalty and your full endeavours to the Popular Front?'

CHRIS: What's the Popular Front?

GERRY: The Spanish government that I'm going to keep in power. 'I take it you are a Syndicalist?' 'No.' 'An Anarchist?' 'No.' 'A Marxist?' 'No.' 'A Republican, a Socialist, a Communist?' 'No.' 'Do you speak Spanish?' 'No.' 'Can you make explosives?' 'No.' 'Can you ride a motor-bike' 'Yes.' 'You're in. Sign here.'

CHRIS: So you'll be a dispatch rider?

(GERRY *imitates riding a motor-bike.*)

And you leave on Saturday?

GERRY: First tide.

CHRIS: How long will you be away?

GERRY: As long as it takes to sort the place out.

CHRIS: Seriously, Gerry.

GERRY: Maybe a couple of months. Everybody says it will be over by Christmas.

CHRIS: They always say it will be over by Christmas. I still don't know why you're going.

GERRY: Not so sure I know either. Who wants salesmen that can't sell? And there's bound to be *something* right about the cause, isn't there? And it's somewhere to go – isn't it? Maybe that's the important thing for a man: a *named* destination – democracy, Ballybeg, heaven. Women's illusions aren't so easily satisfied – they make better drifters. (*Laughs.*) Anyhow he held out a pen to sign on the dotted line and it was only when I was writing my name that I glanced over the lectern and saw the box.

CHRIS: What box?

GERRY: He was standing on a box. The chappie was a midget!

CHRIS: Gerry!

GERRY: No bigger than three feet.

CHRIS: Gerry, I –

GERRY: Promise you! And when we were having a drink afterwards he told me he was invaluable to the Brigade – because he was a master at disguising himself!

CHRIS: Gerry Evans, you are –

GERRY: Let's go down to the old well.

CHRIS: We're going nowhere. Come inside and take a look at this wireless. It stops and starts whenever it feels like it.

GERRY: I told you: I know nothing about radios.

CHRIS: I've said you're a genius at them.

GERRY: Chrissie, I don't even know how to –

CHRIS: You can try, can't you? Come on. Michael misses it badly. (*She runs into the kitchen. He follows.*)
You should see Jack striding through the meadow. He looks like a new man.

KATE: (*To* GERRY) Were you talking to him?

GERRY: He wants to do a swap with me: I'm to give him this hat and he's to give me some sort of a three-cornered hat with feathers that the district commissioner gave him. Sounds a fair exchange.

MAGGIE: Chrissie says you're great with radios, Gerry.

GERRY: I'll take a look at it – why not?

MAGGIE: All I can tell you is that it's not the battery. I got a new one yesterday.

GERRY: Let me check the aerial first. Very often that's where the trouble lies. Then I'll have a look at the ignition and sparking plugs. Leave it to Gerry.

(*He winks at* CHRIS *as he goes out the front door and off right.*)

MAGGIE: He sounds very knowledgeable.

CHRIS: It may be something he can't fix.

KATE: I know you're not responsible for Gerry's decisions, Christina. But it would be on my conscience if I didn't tell you how strongly I disapprove of this International Brigade caper. It's a sorry day for Ireland when we send young men off to Spain to fight for godless Communism.

CHRIS: For democracy, Kate.

KATE: I'm not going to argue. I just want to clear my conscience.

CHRIS: That's the important thing, of course. And now you've cleared it.

(GERRY *runs on and calls through the window:*)

GERRY: Turn the radio on, Chrissie, would you?

MAGGIE: It's on.

GERRY: Right.

(*He runs off again.*)

CHRIS: Just as we were coming out of the town we met Vera McLaughlin, the knitting agent. (*Softly*) Agnes and Rose aren't back yet?

MAGGIE: They'll be here soon.

CHRIS: She says she'll call in tomorrow and tell them herself. The poor woman was very distressed.

KATE: Tell them what?

CHRIS: She's not buying any more hand-made gloves.

MAGGIE: Why not?

CHRIS: Too dear, she says.

KATE: Too dear! She pays them a pittance!

CHRIS: There's a new factory started up in Donegal Town. They

make machine gloves more quickly there and far more
cheaply. The people Vera used to supply buy their gloves
direct from the factory now.

MAGGIE: That's awful news, Chrissie.

CHRIS: She says they're organizing buses to bring the workers to
the factory and back every day. Most of the people who used
to work at home have signed on. She tried to get a job there
herself. They told her she was too old. She's forty-one. The
poor woman could hardly speak.

MAGGIE: Oh God . . . poor Aggie . . . poor Rose . . . what'll they
do?

(AGNES *enters the garden.* KATE *sees her.*)

KATE: Shhh. They're back. Let them have their tea in peace. Tell
them later.

(*They busy themselves with their tasks.* AGNES *is carrying two
small pails of blackberries which she leaves outside the door of the
house. Just as she is about to enter the kitchen a voice off calls
her:*)

GERRY: (*Off*) Who is that beautiful woman!

(*She looks around, puzzled.*)

AGNES: Gerry?

GERRY: Up here, Aggie!

AGNES: Where?

GERRY: On top of the sycamore.

(*Now she sees him. The audience does not see him.*)

AGNES: Mother of God!

GERRY: Come up and join me!

AGNES: What are you doing up there?

GERRY: You can see into the future from here, Aggie!

AGNES: The tree isn't safe, Gerry. Please come down.

GERRY: Come up and see what's going to happen to you!

AGNES: That branch is dead, Gerry. I'm telling you.

(*The branch begins to sway.*)

GERRY: Do you think I could get a job in a circus? Wow-wow-
wow-wow!

AGNES: Gerry – !

GERRY: (*Sings:*) 'He flies through the air with the greatest of
ease – ' Wheeeeeeeeee!

(*She covers her eyes in terror.*)

53

AGNES: Stop it, Gerry, stop it, stop it!

GERRY: 'That daring young man on the flying trapeze . . .'

AGNES: You're going to fall! I'm not looking! I'm not watching!
(*She dashes into the house.*)
That clown of a man is up on top of the sycamore. Go out and tell him to come down, Chrissie.

MAGGIE: He's fixing the aerial.

AGNES: He's going to break his neck – I'm telling you!

MAGGIE: As long as he fixes the wireless first.

KATE: How are the bilberries, Agnes?

AGNES: Just that bit too ripe. We should have picked them a week ago.

CHRIS: Is that a purple stain on your gansey?

AGNES: I know. I'd only begun when I fell into a bush. And look at my hands – all scrabbed with briars. For all the sympathy I got from Rosie. Nearly died laughing at me. How is she now? (*Pause.*) Is she still in bed?

CHRIS: Bed?

AGNES: She wasn't feeling well. She left me and went home to lie down. (*Pause.*) She's here, isn't she?
(MAGGIE *rushes off to the bedroom.*)

KATE: I haven't seen her. (*To* CHRIS) Have you?

CHRIS: No.

KATE: When did she leave you?

AGNES: Hours ago – I don't know – almost immediately after we got to the old quarry. She said she felt out of sorts.

CHRIS: And she went off by herself?

AGNES: Yes.

KATE: To come home?

AGNES: That's what she said.
(MAGGIE *enters.*)

MAGGIE: She's not in her bed.

AGNES: Oh God! Where could she –

KATE: Start at the beginning, Agnes. What exactly happened?

AGNES: Nothing 'happened' – nothing at all. We left here together – when was it? – just after one o'clock –

CHRIS: That means she's missing for over three hours.

AGNES: We walked together to the quarry. She was chatting away as usual. I had my two buckets and she had –

KATE: Go on – go on!

AGNES: And just after we got there she said she wasn't feeling well. I told her not to bother about the bilberries – just to sit in the sun. And that's what she did.

KATE: For how long?

AGNES: I don't know – five – ten minutes. And then I fell into the bush. And that was when she laughed. And then she said – she said – I've forgotten what she said – something about a headache and her stomach being sick and she'd go home and sleep for a while. (*To* MAGGIE) You're sure she's not in her bed?

(MAGGIE *shakes her head*.)

KATE: Then what?

(AGNES *begins to cry*.)

AGNES: Where is she? What's happened to our Rosie?

KATE: What direction did she go when she left you?

AGNES: Direction?

KATE: Stop snivelling, Agnes! Did she go towards home?

AGNES: I think so . . . yes . . . I don't know . . . Maggie –

MAGGIE: She may have gone into the town.

CHRIS: She wouldn't have gone into town in her wellingtons.

AGNES: She was wearing her good shoes.

KATE: Are you sure?

AGNES: Yes; and her blue cardigan and her good skirt. I said to her – I said, 'You're some lady to go picking bilberries with.' And she just laughed and said, 'I'm some toff, Aggie, amn't I some toff?'

MAGGIE: Had she a bottle of milk with her?

AGNES: I think so – yes – in one of her cans.

MAGGIE: Had she any money with her?

AGNES: She had half-a-crown. That's all she has.

MAGGIE: (*Softly*) Danny Bradley.

KATE: What? – who?

MAGGIE: Danny Bradley . . . Lough Anna . . . up in the back hills.

CHRIS: Oh God, no.

KATE: What? – what's this? – what about the back hills?

CHRIS: She has some silly notion about that scamp, Bradley. She believes he's in love with her. He gave her a present last Christmas – she says.

55

KATE: (*To* AGNES) What do you know about this Bradley business?

AGNES: I know no more than Chris has –

KATE: I've often seen you and Rose whispering together. What plot has been hatched between Rose and Mr Bradley?

AGNES: No plot . . . please, Kate –

KATE: You're lying to me, Agnes! You're withholding! I want the truth!

AGNES: Honest to God, all I know is what Chris has just –

KATE: I want to know everything you know! Now! I want to –

MAGGIE: That'll do, Kate! Stop that at once! (*Calmly*) She may be in the town. She may be on her way home now. She may have taken a weak turn on her way back from the quarry. We're going to find her. (*To* CHRIS) You search the fields on the upper side of the lane. (*To* AGNES) You take the lower side, down as far as the main road. (*To* KATE) You go to the old well and search all around there. I'm going into the town to tell the police.

KATE: You're going to no police, Maggie. If she's mixed up with that Bradley creature, I'm not going to have it broadcast all over –

MAGGIE: I'm going to the police and you'll do what I told you to do.

CHRIS: There she is! Look – look! There she is!

(*She has seen* ROSE *through the window and is about to rush out to greet her.* MAGGIE *catches her arm and restrains her. The four sisters watch* ROSE *as she crosses the garden –* CHRIS *and* KATE *from the window,* MAGGIE *and* AGNES *from the door.* ROSE *is unaware of their anxious scrutiny. She is dressed in the 'good' clothes described by* AGNES *and they have changed her appearance. Indeed, had we not seen the* ROSE *of Act 1, we might not now be immediately aware of her disability. At first look this might be any youngish country woman, carefully dressed, not unattractive, returning from a long walk on a summer day. She walks slowly, lethargically, towards the house. From her right hand hangs a red poppy that she plucked casually along the road. Her face reveals nothing – but nothing is being deliberately concealed. She sees Agnes's cans of fruit. She stops beside them and looks at them. Then she puts her hand into one of*)

56

the cans, takes a fistful of berries and thrusts the fistful into her
mouth. Then she wipes her mouth with her sleeve and the back of
her hand. As she chews she looks at her stained fingers. She wipes
them on her skirt. All of these movements – stopping, eating,
wiping – are done not dreamily, abstractedly, but calmly,
naturally. Now she moves towards the house. As she approaches
the door AGNES *rushes to meet her. Instead of hugging her, as she*
wants to, she catches her arm.)

AGNES: Rosie, love, we were beginning to get worried about you.

ROSE: They're nice, Aggie. They're sweet. And you got two
canfuls. Good for you.

(AGNES *leads her into the house.*)

AGNES: Is your stomach settled?

ROSE: My stomach?

AGNES: You weren't feeling well – remember? – when we were at
the quarry?

ROSE: Oh, yes. Oh, I'm fine now, thanks.

AGNES: You left me there and you said you were coming home to
lie down. D'you remember that?

ROSE: Yes.

CHRIS: But you didn't come home, Rosie.

ROSE: That's right.

AGNES: And we were very worried about you.

ROSE: Well . . . here I am.

CHRIS: Were you in the town?

AGNES: That's why you're all dressed up, isn't it?

CHRIS: You went into Ballybeg, didn't you?

(*Pause.* ROSE *looks from one to the other.*)

MAGGIE: (*Briskly*) She's home safe and sound and that's all that
matters. Now I don't know about you girls but I can tell you
this chicken is weak with hunger. Let me tell you what's on
the menu this evening. Our beverage is the usual hot, sweet
tea. There is a choice between caraway-seed bread and soda
bread, both fresh from the chef's oven. But now we come to
the difficulty: there's only three eggs between the seven of us
– I wish to God you'd persuade that white rooster of yours to
lay eggs, Rosie.

CHRIS: There are eight of us, Maggie.

MAGGIE: How are there – ? Of course – the soldier up the

sycamore! Not a great larder but a nice challenge to someone like myself. Right. My suggestion is . . . Eggs Ballybeg; in other words scrambled and served on lightly toasted caraway-seed bread. Followed – for those so inclined – by one magnificent Wild Woodbine. Everybody happy?

CHRIS: Excellent, Margaret!

MAGGIE: Settled.

(ROSE *has taken off her shoe and is examining it carefully*.)

AGNES: We'll go and pick some more bilberries next Sunday, Rosie.

ROSE: All right.

AGNES: Remember the cans you had? You had your own two cans – remember? Did you take them with you?

ROSE: Where to, Aggie?

AGNES: Into the town . . . wherever you went . . .

ROSE: I hid them at the quarry behind a stone wall. They're safe there. I'll go back and pick them up later this evening. Does anybody know where my overall is?

MAGGIE: It's lying across your bed. And you'd need to bring some turf in, Rosie.

ROSE: I'll change first, Maggie.

MAGGIE: Be quick about it.

CHRIS: How many pieces of toast do you want?

MAGGIE: All that loaf. And go easy on the butter – that's all we have. Now. Parsley. And just a whiff of basil. I don't want you to be too optimistic, girls, but you should know I feel very creative this evening.

(ROSE *moves towards the bedroom door. Just as she is about to exit:*)

KATE: I want to know where you have been, Rose.

(ROSE *stops. Pause.*)

You have been gone for the entire afternoon. I want you to tell me where you've been.

AGNES: Later, Kate; after –

KATE: Where have you been for the past three hours?

ROSE: (*Inaudible*) Lough Anna.

KATE: I didn't hear what you said, Rose.

ROSE: Lough Anna.

CHRIS: Kate, just leave –

58

KATE: You walked from the quarry to Lough Anna?

ROSE: Yes.

KATE: Did you meet somebody there?

ROSE: Yes.

KATE: Had you arranged to meet somebody there?

ROSE: I had arranged to meet Danny Bradley there, Kate. He brought me out in his father's blue boat. (*To* MAGGIE) I don't want anything to eat, Maggie. I brought a bottle of milk and a packet of chocolate biscuits with me and we had a picnic on the lake. (*To* AGNES) Then the two of us went up through the back hills. He showed me what was left of the Lughnasa fires. A few of them are still burning away up there. (*To* KATE) We passed young Sweeney's house – you know, the boy who got burned, the boy you said was dying. Well, he's on the mend, Danny says. His legs will be scarred but he'll be all right. (*To all*) It's a very peaceful place up there. There was nobody there but Danny and me. (*To* AGNES) He calls me his Rosebud, Aggie. I told you that before, didn't I? (*To all*) Then he walked me down as far as the workhouse gate and I came on home by myself. (*To* KATE) And that's all I'm going to tell you. (*To all*) That's all any of you are going to hear.

(*She exits, her shoes in one hand, the poppy in the other*. MICHAEL *enters*.)

KATE: What has happened to this house? Mother of God, will we ever be able to lift our heads ever again . . . ?

(*Pause*.)

MICHAEL: The following night Vera McLaughlin arrived and explained to Agnes and Rose why she couldn't buy their hand-knitted gloves any more. Most of her home knitters were already working in the new factory and she advised Agnes and Rose to apply immediately. The Industrial Revolution had finally caught up with Ballybeg.

They didn't apply, even though they had no other means of making a living, and they never discussed their situation with their sisters. Perhaps Agnes made the decision for both of them because she knew Rose wouldn't have got work there anyway. Or perhaps, as Kate believed, because Agnes was too notionate to work in a factory. Or perhaps the two of them just wanted . . . away.

Anyhow, on my first day back at school, when we came into the kitchen for breakfast, there was a note propped up against the milk jug: 'We are gone for good. This is best for all. Do not try to find us.' It was written in Agnes's resolute hand.

Of course they did try to find them. So did the police. So did our neighbours who had a huge network of relatives all over England and America. But they had vanished without trace. And by the time I tracked them down – twenty-five years later, in London – Agnes was dead and Rose was dying in a hospice for the destitute in Southwark.

The scraps of information I gathered about their lives during those missing years were too sparse to be coherent. They had moved about a lot. They had worked as cleaning women in public toilets, in factories, in the Underground. Then, when Rose could no longer get work, Agnes tried to support them both – but couldn't. From then on, I gathered, they gave up. They took to drink; slept in parks, in doorways, on the Thames Embankment. Then Agnes died of exposure. And two days after I found Rose in that grim hospice – she didn't recognize me, of course – she died in her sleep.

Father Jack's health improved quickly and he soon recovered his full vocabulary and all his old bounce and vigour. But he didn't say Mass that following Monday. In fact he never said Mass again. And the neighbours stopped enquiring about him. And his name never again appeared in the *Donegal Enquirer*. And of course there was never a civic reception with bands and flags and speeches.

But he never lost his determination to return to Uganda and he still talked passionately about his life with the lepers there. And each new anecdote contained more revelations. And each new revelation startled – shocked – stunned poor Aunt Kate. Until finally she hit on a phrase that appeased her: 'his own distinctive spiritual search'. 'Leaping around a fire and offering a little hen to Uka or Ito or whoever is not religion as I was taught it and indeed know it,' she would say with a defiant toss of her head. 'But then Jack must make his own distinctive search.' And when he died suddenly of a heart attack – within a year of his homecoming, on the very eve of the following Lá Lughnasa – my mother and Maggie mourned him sorely. But for months Kate was inconsolable.

My father sailed for Spain that Saturday. The last I saw of him was dancing down the lane in imitation of Fred Astaire, swinging his walking stick, Uncle Jack's ceremonial tricorn at a jaunty angle over his left eye. When he got to the main road he stopped and turned and with both hands blew a dozen theatrical kisses back to Mother and me.

He was wounded in Barcelona – he fell off his motor-bike – so that for the rest of his life he walked with a limp. The limp wasn't disabling but it put an end to his dancing days; and that really distressed him. Even the role of maimed veteran, which he loved, could never compensate for that.

He still visited us occasionally, perhaps once a year. Each time he was on the brink of a new career. And each time he proposed to Mother and promised me a new bike. Then the war came in 1939; his visits became more infrequent; and finally he stopped coming altogether.

Sometime in the mid-fifties I got a letter from a tiny village in the south of Wales; a curt note from a young man of my own age and also called Michael Evans. He had found my name and address among the belongings of his father, Gerry Evans. He introduced himself as my half-brother and he wanted me to know that Gerry Evans, the father we shared, had died peacefully in the family home the previous week. Throughout his final illness he was nursed by his wife and his three grown children who all lived and worked in the village.

My mother never knew of that letter. I decided to tell her – decided not to – vacillated for years as my father would have done; and eventually, rightly or wrongly, kept the information to myself.

(MAGGIE, CHRIS, KATE *and* AGNES *now resume their tasks.*)

CHRIS: Well, at least that's good news.

MAGGIE: What's that?

CHRIS: That the young Sweeney boy from the back hills is going to live.

MAGGIE: Good news indeed.

(CHRIS *goes to the door and calls:*)

CHRIS: Michael! Where are you? We need some turf brought in!

(*She now goes outside and calls up to* GERRY. MICHAEL *exits.*)
Are you still up there?

GERRY: (*Off*) Don't stand there. I might fall on top of you.

CHRIS: Have you any idea what you're doing?

GERRY: (*Off*) Come on up here to me.

CHRIS: I'm sure I will.

GERRY: (*Off*) We never made love on top of a sycamore tree.
(*She looks quickly around: did her sisters hear that?*)

CHRIS: If you fall and break your neck it'll be too good for you.
(*She goes inside.*) Nobody can vanish quicker than that
Michael fellow when you need him.

MAGGIE: (*To* AGNES) I had a brilliant idea when I woke up this
morning, Aggie. I thought to myself: what is it that Ballybeg
badly needs and that Ballybeg hasn't got?

AGNES: A riddle. Give up.

MAGGIE: A dressmaker! So why doesn't Agnes Mundy who has
such clever hands, why doesn't she dressmake?

AGNES: Clever hands!
(MAGGIE *looks around for her cigarettes.*)

MAGGIE: She'd get a pile of work. They'd come to her from far
and wide. She'd make a fortune.

AGNES: Some fortune in Ballybeg.

MAGGIE: And not only would the work be interesting but she
wouldn't be ruining her eyes staring at grey wool eight hours
a day. Did you notice how Rosie squints at things now? It's
the job for you, Aggie; I'm telling you. Ah, holy God, girls,
don't tell me I'm out of fags! How could that have happened?
(CHRIS *goes to the mantelpiece and produces a single cigarette.*)
Chrissie, you are one genius. Look, Kate. (*Scowls.*) Misery.
(*Lights cigarette.*) Happiness! Want a drag?

KATE: What's keeping those wonderful Eggs Ballybeg?

MAGGIE: If I had to choose between one Wild Woodbine and a
man of – say – fifty-two – widower – plump, what would I
do, Kate? I'd take fatso, wouldn't I? God, I really am getting
desperate.
(JACK *enters through the garden.*)
Maybe I should go to Ryanga with you, Jack.

JACK: I know you won't but I know you'd love it.

MAGGIE: Could you guarantee a man for each of us?

JACK: I couldn't promise four men but I should be able to get one husband for all of you.

MAGGIE: Would we settle for that?

CHRIS: One between the four of us?

JACK: That's our system and it works very well. One of you would be his principal wife and live with him in his largest hut –

MAGGIE: That'd be you, Kate.

KATE: Stop that, Maggie!

JACK: And the other three of you he'd keep in his enclosure. It would be like living on the same small farm.

MAGGIE: Snug enough, girls, isn't it? (*To* JACK) And what would be – what sort of duties would we have?

JACK: Cooking, sewing, helping with the crops, washing – the usual housekeeping tasks.

MAGGIE: Sure that's what we do anyway.

JACK: And looking after his children.

MAGGIE: That he'd have by Kate.

KATE: Maggie!

JACK: By all four of you! And what's so efficient about that system is that the husband and his wives and his children make up a small commune where everybody helps everybody else and cares for them. I'm completely in favour of it.

KATE: It may be efficient and you may be in favour of it, Jack, but I don't think it's what Pope Pius XI considers to be the holy sacrament of matrimony. And it might be better for you if you paid just a bit more attention to our Holy Father and a bit less to the Great Goddess . . . Iggie.

(*Music of 'Anything Goes' very softly on the radio.*)

CHRIS: Listen.

MAGGIE: And they have hens there, too, Jack?

JACK: We're overrun with hens.

MAGGIE: Don't dismiss it, girls. It has its points. Would you be game, Kate?

KATE: Would you give my head peace, Maggie.

CHRIS: Gerry has it going!

MAGGIE: Tell me this, Jack: what's the Swahili for 'tchook-tchook-tchook-tchook-tchook'?

JACK: You'd love the climate, too, Kate.

KATE: I'm not listening to a word you're saying.

(GERRY *runs on*.)

GERRY: Well? Any good?

CHRIS: Listen.

GERRY: Aha. Leave it to the expert.

JACK: I have something for you, Gerry.

GERRY: What's that?

JACK: The plumed hat – the ceremonial hat – remember? We agreed to swap. With you in a second.

(*He goes to his bedroom*.)

MAGGIE: Good work, Gerry.

GERRY: Thought it might be the aerial. That's the end of your troubles. (*Listens. Sings a line of the song*.) Dance with me, Agnes.

AGNES: Have a bit of sense, Gerry Evans.

GERRY: Dance with me. Please. Come on.

MAGGIE: Dance with him, Aggie.

GERRY: (*Sings:*) 'In olden times a glimpse of stocking
    Was looked on as something shocking – '
Give me your hand.

MAGGIE: Go on, Aggie.

AGNES: Who wants to dance at this time of –

(GERRY *pulls her to her feet and takes her in his arms*.)

GERRY: (*Sings:*) '. . . anything goes.
    Good authors, too, who once knew better words
    Now only use four-letter words
    Writing prose,
    Anything goes . . .'

(*Bring up the sound. With style and with easy elegance they dance once around the kitchen and then out to the garden –* GERRY *singing the words directly to her face:*)

    If driving fast cars you like,
    If low bars you like,
    If old hymns you like,
    If bare limbs you like,
    If Mae West you like,
    Or me undressed you like,
    Why, nobody will oppose.
    When ev'ry night, the set that's smart is in-
    truding in nudist parties in

64

Studios,
Anything goes . . .'
(*They are now in the far corner of the garden.*)
You're a great dancer, Aggie.
AGNES: No, I'm not.
GERRY: You're a superb dancer.
AGNES: No, I'm not.
GERRY: You should be a professional dancer.
AGNES: Too late for that.
GERRY: You could teach dancing in Ballybeg.
AGNES: That's all they need.
GERRY: Maybe it is!
(*He bends down and kisses her on the forehead. All this is seen –
but not heard – by* CHRIS *at the kitchen window. Immediately
after this kiss* GERRY *bursts into song again, turns* AGNES *four or
five times very rapidly and dances her back to the kitchen.*)
There you are. Safe and sound.
MAGGIE: I wish to God I could dance like you, Aggie.
AGNES: I haven't a breath.
GERRY: Doesn't she dance elegantly?
MAGGIE: Always did, our Aggie.
GERRY: Unbelievable. Now, Chrissie – you and I.
CHRIS: (*Sharply*) Not now. I wonder where Michael's got to?
GERRY: Come on, Chrissie. Once round the floor.
CHRIS: Not now, I said. Are you thick?
MAGGIE: I'll dance with you, Gerry! (*She kicks her wellingtons off.*)
Do you want to see real class?
GERRY: Certainly do, Maggie.
MAGGIE: Stand back there, girls. Shirley Temple needs a lot of space.
GERRY: Wow-wow-wow-wow!
MAGGIE: Hold me close, Gerry. The old legs aren't too reliable.
(*She and* GERRY *sing and dance:*)
'In olden times a glimpse of stocking
Was looked on as something shocking
But now –'
(CHRIS *suddenly turns the radio off.*)
CHRIS: Sick of that damned thing.
GERRY: What happened?
MAGGIE: What are you at there, Chrissie?

CHRIS: We're only wasting the battery and we won't get a new one until the weekend.

MAGGIE: It wasn't to be, Gerry. But there'll be another day.

GERRY: That's a promise, Maggie.
(*He goes to* CHRIS *at the radio.*)
Not a bad little set, that.

KATE: Peace, thanks be to God! D'you know what that thing has done? Killed all Christian conversation in this country.

CHRIS: (*To* AGNES, *icily*) Vera McLaughlin's calling here tomorrow. She wants to talk to you and Rose.

AGNES: What about?

KATE: (*Quickly*) I didn't tell you, did I? – her daughter's got engaged!

MAGGIE: Which of them?

KATE: 'The harvest dance is going to be just supreme this year, Miss Mundy' – that wee brat!

MAGGIE: Sophia. Is she not still at school?

KATE: Left last year. She's fifteen. And the lucky man is sixteen.

MAGGIE: Holy God. We may pack it in, girls.

KATE: It's indecent, I'm telling you. Fifteen and sixteen! Don't tell me that's not totally improper. It's the poor mother I feel sorry for.

AGNES: What does she want to talk to us about?

CHRIS: (*Relenting*) Something about wool. Didn't sound important. She probably won't call at all.
(CHRIS *turns the radio on again. No sound.*)
(*To* MAGGIE) Go ahead and dance, you two.

MAGGIE: Artistes like Margaret Mundy can't perform on demand, Chrissie. We need to be in touch with other forces first, don't we, Gerry?

GERRY: Absolutely. Why is there no sound?

KATE: Maggie, are we never going to eat?

MAGGIE: Indeed we are – outside in the garden! Eggs Ballybeg *al fresco*. Lughnasa's almost over, girls. There aren't going to be many warm evenings left.

KATE: Good idea, Maggie.

AGNES: I'll get the cups and plates.

GERRY: (*With* CHRIS *at radio*) Are you all right?

CHRIS: It's not gone again, is it?

66

GERRY: Have I done something wrong?

CHRIS: I switched it on again – that's all I did.

MAGGIE: Take out those chairs, Gerry.

GERRY: What about the table?

MAGGIE: We'll just spread a cloth on the ground.

(MAGGIE *exits with the cloth which she spreads in the middle of the garden.* GERRY *kisses* CHRIS *lightly on the back of the neck.*)

GERRY: At least we know it's not the aerial.

CHRIS: According to you.

GERRY: And if it's not the aerial the next thing to check is the ignition.

CHRIS: Ignition! Listen to that bluffer!

GERRY: Bluffer? (*To* AGNES *as she passes*) Did you hear what she called me? That's unfair, Agnes, isn't it?

(AGNES *smiles and shrugs.*)

Let's take the back off and see what's what.

(ROSE *enters the garden from the back of the house. At first nobody notices her. She is dressed as in Act 1. In her right hand she holds the dead rooster by the feet. Its feathers are ruffled and it is stained with blood.* ROSE *is calm, almost matter-of-fact.* AGNES *sees her first and goes to her.* CHRIS *and* GERRY *join the others in the garden.*)

AGNES: Rosie, what is it, Rosie?

ROSE: My rooster's dead.

AGNES: Oh Rosie . . .

ROSE: (*Holding the dead bird up*) Look at him. He's dead.

AGNES: What happened to him?

ROSE: The fox must have got him.

AGNES: Oh, poor Rosie . . .

ROSE: Maggie warned me the fox was about again. (*To all*) That's the end of my pet rooster. The fox must have got him. You were right, Maggie.

(*She places it carefully on the tablecloth in the middle of the garden.*)

MAGGIE: Did he get at the hens?

ROSE: I don't think so.

MAGGIE: Was the door left open?

ROSE: They're all right. They're safe.

MAGGIE: That itself.

AGNES: We'll get another white rooster for you, Rosie.

ROSE: Doesn't matter.

MAGGIE: And I'll put manners on him early on.

ROSE: I don't want another.

MAGGIE: (*Quick hug*) Poor old Rosie. (*As she moves away*) We can hardly expect him to lay for us now . . .

CHRIS: Where's that Michael fellow got to? Michael! He hears me rightly, you know. I'm sure he's jouking about out there somewhere, watching us. Michael!

(ROSE *sits on the garden seat.*)

MAGGIE: All right, girls, what's missing? Knives, forks, plates –

(*She sees* JACK *coming through the kitchen.*)

Jesus, Mary and Joseph!

(JACK *is wearing a very soiled, very crumpled white uniform – a version of the uniform we saw him in at the very beginning of the play. One of the epaulettes is hanging by a thread and the gold buttons are tarnished. The uniform is so large that it looks as if it were made for a much larger man: his hands are lost in the sleeves and the trousers trail on the ground. On his head he wears a tricorn, ceremonial hat; once white like the uniform but now grubby, the plumage broken and tatty. He carries himself in military style, his army cane under his arm.*)

JACK: Gerry, my friend, where are you?

GERRY: Out here, Jack.

JACK: There you are. (*To all*) I put on my ceremonial clothes for the formal exchange. There was a time when it fitted me – believe it or not. Wonderful uniform, isn't it?

GERRY: Unbelievable. I could do with that for Spain.

JACK: It was my uniform when I was chaplain to the British army during the Great War.

KATE: We know only too well what it is, Jack.

JACK: Isn't it splendid? Well, it was splendid. Needs a bit of a clean up. Okawa's always dressing up in it. I really must give it to him to keep.

KATE: It's not at all suitable for this climate, Jack.

JACK: You're right, Kate. Just for the ceremony – then I'll change back. Now, if I were at home, what we do when we swap or barter is this. I place my possession on the ground –

(*He and* GERRY *enact this ritual.*)

Go ahead. (*Of hat*) Put it on the grass – anywhere – just at your feet. Now take three steps away from it – yes? – a symbolic distancing of yourself from what you once possessed. Good. Now turn round once – like this – yes, a complete circle – and that's the formal rejection of what you once had – you no longer lay claim to it. Now I cross over to where you stand – right? And you come over to the position I have left. So. Excellent. The exchange is now formally and irrevocably complete. This is my straw hat. And that is your tricorn hat. Put it on. Splendid! And it suits you! Doesn't it suit him?

CHRIS: His head's too big.

GERRY: (*Adjusting hat*) What about that? (*To* AGNES) is that better, Agnes?

AGNES: You're lovely.

(GERRY *does a Charlie Chaplin walk across the garden, his feet spread, his cane twirling. As he does he sings:*)

GERRY: 'In olden times a glimpse of stocking
       Was looked on as something shocking . . .'

JACK: (*Adjusting his hat*) And what about this? Or like this? Or further back on my head?

MAGGIE: Would you look at them! Strutting about like a pair of peacocks! Now – teatime!

AGNES: I'll make the tea.

MAGGIE: You can start again tomorrow. Let me finish off Lughnasa. Chrissie, put on Marconi.

CHRIS: I think it's broken again.

AGNES: Gerry fixed it. Didn't you?

GERRY: Then Chrissie got at it again.

CHRIS: Possessed that thing, if you ask me.

KATE: I wish you wouldn't use words like that, Christina. There's still great heat in that sun.

MAGGIE: Great harvest weather.

KATE: I love September.

MAGGIE: (*Not moving*) Cooking time, girls.

KATE: Wait a while, Maggie. Enjoy the bit of heat that's left.

(AGNES *moves beside* ROSE.)

AGNES: Next Sunday, then. Is that all right?

ROSE: What's next Sunday?

AGNES: We'll get some more bilberries.

69

ROSE: Yes. Yes. Whatever you say, Aggie.
  (GERRY *examines the kites.*)
GERRY: Not bad for a kid of seven. Very neatly made.
KATE: Look at the artwork.
GERRY: Wow-wow-wow-wow! That is unbelievable!
KATE: I keep telling his mother – she has a very talented son.
CHRIS: So there, Mr Evans.
GERRY: Have you all seen these?
MAGGIE: I hate them.
GERRY: I think they're just wonderful. Look, Jack.
  (*For the first time we all see the images. On each kite is painted a
  crude, cruel, grinning face, primitively drawn, garishly painted.*)
  I'll tell you something: this boy isn't going to end up selling
  gramophones.
CHRIS: Michael! He always vanishes when there's work to be
  done.
MAGGIE: I've a riddle for you. Why is a gramophone like a
  parrot?
KATE: Maggie!
MAGGIE: Because it . . . because it always . . . because a parrot
  . . . God, I've forgotten!
  (MAGGIE *moves into the kitchen.* MICHAEL *enters. The
  characters are now in positions similar to their positions at the
  beginning of the play – with some changes:* AGNES *and* GERRY
  are on the garden seat. JACK *stands stiffly to attention at Agnes's
  elbow. One kite, facing boldly out front, stands between* GERRY
  and AGNES; *the other between* AGNES *and* JACK. ROSE *is
  upstage left.* MAGGIE *is at the kitchen window.* KATE *is
  downstage right.* CHRIS *is at the front door. During* MICHAEL's
  speech KATE *cries quietly. As* MICHAEL *begins to speak the stage
  is lit in a very soft, golden light so that the tableau we see is
  almost, but not quite, in a haze.*)
MICHAEL: As I said, Father Jack was dead within twelve months.
  And with him and Agnes and Rose all gone, the heart seemed
  to go out of the house.
    Maggie took on the tasks Rose and Agnes had done and
  pretended to believe that nothing had changed. My mother
  spent the rest of her life in the knitting factory – and hated
  every day of it. And after a few years doing nothing Kate got

the job of tutoring the young family of Austin Morgan of the Arcade. But much of the spirit and fun had gone out of their lives; and when my time came to go away, in the selfish way of young men I was happy to escape.

(*Now fade in very softly, just audible, the music – 'It is Time to Say Goodnight' (not from the radio speaker).*

And as MICHAEL *continues everybody sways very slightly from side to side – even the grinning kites. The movement is so minimal that we cannot be quite certain if it is happening or if we imagine it.*)

And so, when I cast my mind back to that summer of 1936, different kinds of memories offer themselves to me.

But there is one memory of that Lughnasa time that visits me most often; and what fascinates me about that memory is that it owes nothing to fact. In that memory atmosphere is more real than incident and everything is simultaneously actual and illusory. In that memory, too, the air is nostalgic with the music of the thirties. It drifts in from somewhere far away – a mirage of sound – a dream music that is both heard and imagined; that seems to be both itself and its own echo; a sound so alluring and so mesmeric that the afternoon is bewitched, maybe haunted, by it. And what is so strange about that memory is that everybody seems to be floating on those sweet sounds, moving rhythmically, languorously, in complete isolation; responding more to the mood of the music than to its beat. When I remember it, I think of it as dancing. Dancing with eyes half closed because to open them would break the spell. Dancing as if language had surrendered to movement – as if this ritual, this wordless ceremony, was now the way to speak, to whisper private and sacred things, to be in touch with some otherness. Dancing as if the very heart of life and all its hopes might be found in those assuaging notes and those hushed rhythms and in those silent and hypnotic movements. Dancing as if language no longer existed because words were no longer necessary . . .

(*Slowly bring up the music. Slowly bring down the lights.*)

THE END